Families
A Social Class Perspective

CONTEMPORARY
FAMILY
PERSPECTIVES

SHIRLEY A. HILL
University of Kansas

Los Angeles | London | New Delhi
Singapore | Washington DC

Los Angeles | London | New Delhi
Singapore | Washington DC

FOR INFORMATION:

SAGE Publications, Inc.

2455 Teller Road

Thousand Oaks, California 91320

E-mail: order@sagepub.com

SAGE Publications Ltd.

1 Oliver's Yard

55 City Road

London EC1Y 1SP

United Kingdom

SAGE Publications India Pvt. Ltd.

B 1/I 1 Mohan Cooperative Industrial Area

Mathura Road, New Delhi 110 044

India

SAGE Publications Asia-Pacific Pte. Ltd.

33 Pekin Street #02-01

Far East Square

Singapore 048763

Acquisitions Editor: David Repetto

Editorial Assistant: Maggie Stanley

Production Editor: Brittany Bauhaus

Copy Editor: Diana Breti

Typesetter: C&M Digitals (P) Ltd.

Proofreader: Sarah Duffy

Indexer: Diggs Publication Services, Inc.

Cover Designer: Janet Kiesel

Marketing Manager: Erica DeLuca

Permissions Editor: Karen Ehrmann

Copyright © 2012 by Pine Forge Press,
an Imprint of SAGE Publications, Inc.

Printed in the United States of America

Library of Congress Cataloging-in-Publication Data

Hill, Shirley A. (Shirley Ann), 1947-

Families : a social class perspective / Shirley A. Hill.

p. cm.
—(Contemporary family perspectives) Includes
bibliographical references.

ISBN 978-1-4129-9801-7 (pbk. : acid-free paper)

1. Families. 2. Social classes.
3. Industrialization. I. Title. II. Series.

HQ503.H55. 2012
306.85086'2—dc22
2011001746

This book is printed on acid-free paper.

11 12 13 14 15 10 9 8 7 6 5 4 3 2 1

Contents

Series Preface

Contemporary Family Perspectives

Susan J. Ferguson
Grinnell College

The family is one of the most private and pervasive social institutions in U.S. society. At the same time, public discussions and debates about the institution of the family persist. Some scholars and public figures claim that the family is declining or dying or that the contemporary family is in crisis or morally deficient. Other scholars argue that the family has been caught in the larger culture wars taking place in the United States. The current debates on legalizing same-sex marriage are one example of this larger public discussion about the institution of the family. Regardless of one's perspective that the family is declining or caught in broader political struggles, scholars agree that the institution has undergone dramatic transformations in recent decades. U.S. demographic data reveal that fewer people are married, divorce rates remain high at almost 50 percent, and more families are living in poverty. In addition, people are creating new kinds of families via Internet dating, cohabitation, single-parent adoption, committed couples living apart, donor insemination, and polyamorous relationships. The demographic data and ethnographic research on new family forms require that family scholars pay attention to a variety of family structures, processes, ideologies, and social norms. In particular, scholars need to address important questions about the family, such as What is the future of marriage? Is divorce harmful to individuals, to the institution of the family, and/or to society? Why are rates of family violence so high? Are we living in a post-dating culture? How do poverty and welfare policies affect families? How is child rearing changing now that so many parents work outside the home and children spend time with caregivers other than their parents? Finally, how are families socially constructed in various societies and cultures?

Most sociologists and family scholars agree that the family is a dynamic social institution that is continually changing as other social structures and individuals in society change. The family also is a social construction, with complex and shifting age, gender, race, and social class meanings. Many excellent studies are currently investigating the changing structures of the institution of the family and the lived experiences and meanings of families. **Contemporary Family Perspectives** is a series of short texts and research monographs that provides a forum for the best of this burgeoning scholarship. The series aims to recognize the diversity of families that exist in the United States and globally. A second goal is for the series to better inform pedagogy and future family scholarship about this diversity of families. The series also seeks to connect family scholarship to a broader audience beyond the classroom by informing the public and by ensuring that family studies remain central to contemporary policy debates and to social action. Each short text contains the most outstanding current scholarship on the family from a variety of disciplines, including sociology, demography, policy studies, social work, human development, and psychology. Moreover, each short text is authored by a leading family scholar or scholars who bring their unique disciplinary perspective to an understanding of contemporary families.

Contemporary Family Perspectives provides the most advanced scholarship and up-to-date findings on the family. Each volume contains a brief overview of significant scholarship on that family topic, including critical current debates or areas of scholarly disagreement. In addition to providing an assessment of the latest findings related to their family topic, authors also examine the family utilizing an intersectional framework of race/ethnicity, social class, gender, and sexuality. Much of the research is interdisciplinary, with a number of theoretical frameworks and methodological approaches presented. Several of the family scholars use a historical lens as well to ground their contemporary research. A particular strength of the series is that the short texts appeal to undergraduate students as well as to family scholars, but they are written in a way that makes them accessible to a larger public.

About This Volume

Social class and social inequality affect families in similar and disparate ways. To date, more family scholarship has focused on poor families and the problems they face than on the social realities of families in other social classes. What makes this book unique is that it provides a comprehensive look at families across social classes in the United States. *Families: A Social Class Perspective* brings together the best scholarship and data available to describe the extent of social class differences among U.S. families and how these social class variations can be historically and theoretically understood. The author, Shirley Hill, a professor of sociology and family scholar at the University of Kansas, draws upon diverse family research to help readers appreciate how social class and the economic structure impact the social organization of families as well as how the lived experiences of social inequality affect families across the social class structure.

Hill begins by examining how social class is defined in the United States and how social inequality affects families. She also reviews the social history of families and how social and economic changes have impacted the institution of the family over time. Hill shows that the economic consequences of industrialization on families are complex and vary by gender and race/ethnicity. Moreover, she encourages readers to think about how different social theories might explain these social class variations in families. After laying this groundwork, Hill investigates marriage, work, and child rearing in three larger social class groupings: upper-class, middle-class, and poor families. Hill concludes by looking at how social inequality affects families in a global context.

Topics covered include the definition and measurement of social class, a historical overview of the family as an institution, theories of social inequality and theories of families, an overview of research on both children and adults in elite and upper-class, middle-class, and economically marginal families, and finally, an overview of families in a global economic context.

Families: A Social Class Perspective is appropriate for use in any class concerned with family structure, social inequality, gender, social welfare, and government policy. This book is a valuable resource to teachers and students in beginning and advanced courses in sociology, psychology, family studies, women's studies, human development, social work, public policy, and other disciplines. It also finds an audience among those who work in various human service fields, including human development, social work, education, counseling, health services, and the government.

Author Preface

Shirley A. Hill

This book examines families using a social class perspective. Social class is arguably the most powerful predictor of many aspects of social life, including the structure and viability of families. Yet many scholars contend that social class awareness remains marginal in American society. People are, of course, aware that some families are wealthy and others poor, with the majority somewhere in between. Fewer, however, understand the causes or consequences of social class inequality, the factors that perpetuate it, or how fundamentally it shapes our family lives. Understanding the implications of social class has historically been obscured by ideologies such as the American Dream—the belief that anyone can achieve success and mobility through hard work and determination—and the belief that the United States is essentially a middle-class society. Although it is the case that the United States developed one of the strongest middle-class societies that has ever existed, a truly equitable society remained elusive. In fact, in recent decades, social class inequalities have intensified, and the United States has the highest level of inequality among advanced industrial societies. The most-documented patterns of expanding social inequality have been the increase in wealth among the wealthy, the growing number of working families that live at or near the poverty level, and the decline in the earnings and economic stability of families in the middle class.

Families: A Social Class Perspective foregrounds the centrality of social class in shaping family life. It starts with an overview of how families have changed since the mid-twentieth century and places those changes in the context of the civil rights and feminist movements of the 1960s and 1970s. The dominant definition of "family" was contested by women and racial minorities as they pushed for greater equality but, I contend, underlying these ideological debates were evolving economic forces that were already challenging the stability of many families. Although there is no immutable correspondence between the economy and the structure of families, I draw on historical trends to show that the two tend to evolve in tandem. Social inequality is as old as humankind, but the social class system of inequality emerged, for the most part, with the industrial economy. American scholars of that era tended to shy away from critical analyses of social inequality but, as I discuss in Chapter 2, a notable shift in theorizing inequalities emerged in the late 1960s. Chapter 2 examines how social theorists analyzed social class and families and includes a discussion of feminist theorists and the shift from a social class approach to a cultural approach to understanding African American families.

In Chapters 3 to 5, I explore family life from a social class perspective. These chapters examine the origins of the elite, middle, and economically marginal classes, along with how family life in each tier is shaped by their social class position. Each chapter includes an analysis of how gender and racial inequalities operate in the context of class inequality. Chapter 6 is devoted to exploring social inequality and families from a broader, global perspective.

I would like to take this opportunity to thank Susan Ferguson, the editor of this series, for inviting me to write this book and supporting me along the way. I extend a note of appreciation to the editors at Sage Publications for their help with this project. Finally, I want to especially thank my husband, Edwin, who supports me in every endeavor and so faithfully proofreads everything I write.

Introduction

Family Studies and Social Inequalities

When I started teaching family sociology in the late 1970s, the field was ablaze with debates over the definition, universality, functionality, and even the need for families. Much of that debate emerged as a critique of the cultural idealization of the American family as a two-parent, nuclear, white, middle-class, suburban entity in which men were the sole wage earners and women devoted their full-time energies to taking care of the home and children. At the core of this idealized notion of family was a heterosexual marriage based on free choice, romantic love, and emotional intimacy—all seen as vital elements for forming a union destined to last a lifetime. Scholars described this family model as the breadwinner-homemaker family and explained that it was a result of nineteenth-century industrialization and modernization, both of which were seen as evolutionary forces that would eventually transform all societies and social institutions. Theorists held that, as social institutions, modern families functioned best when they were nuclear in structure, had a clear gender division of labor, and specialized in rearing children and meeting the emotional needs of adults. The rise of other modern specialized institutions, such as hospitals, led theorists to argue that families should relinquish many of their earlier functions, such as caring for the sick, educating children, and producing food. In the United States, this family ideology reached its zenith as a cultural norm after World War II when soldiers returned home, families were reunited, economic growth spiraled, and the middle class grew. The breadwinner-homemaker family model came to epitomize modernity and socioeconomic success; for example, it was immortalized in popular television shows, such as *Leave It to Beaver* and *Ozzie and Harriet,* and is still idealized by many people as the "traditional family."

Yet, there were millions of families who were unable to conform to the breadwinner-homemaker family model, despite it being endorsed by scholars and popularized by the media as the norm for American families. Moreover, this family model was relatively short-lived: By the 1970s, families were undergoing rapid transformations. It was during that decade, for example, that the rate of divorce exceeded the rate of marriage for the first time in history, and, in the ensuing decades, nonmarital childbearing, cohabitation, dual-income families, and single parenthood became much more common. The pace of family change now has stabilized, but its impact endures. Today, marriages are delayed, one-half of new marriages end in divorce, nearly 40 percent of children are born to unmarried couples, millions of couples opt for nonmarital cohabitation before or instead of marriage, and same-sex couples enter legalized civil unions even as they contend for the same marital rights accorded to heterosexual couples. Families changed dramatically during the last decades of the twentieth century, and, as these changes unfolded, the breadwinner-homemaker family model became a lightning rod for debates over what constituted a viable family and why families were changing. Within this context, the once-idealized *Leave It to Beaver* family was transformed from the dominant cultural ideal to a symbol of how scholars and the media had ignored issues such as the racial/ethnic diversity of families, the oppressive aspects of family life for women, and social class inequality.

Underlying this critique of the family and significant changes in families were economic transitions that were making it more difficult to create male wage-earner families and the emergence of social protest movements that challenged traditions and laws that supported racial/ethnic and gender inequality. Even amid the economic affluence of the 1950s, economists were predicting the demise of the industrial economy, which would mean the loss of high-paying, male-dominated jobs and the creation of an underclass of marginally and/or unemployed men (Gans 1995). The creation of the post-industrial information and services economy resulted in a proliferation of female-typed jobs that increasingly drew women into the labor market, yet most found themselves confined to low-paying jobs and accused of prioritizing labor market work over family. African Americans were migrating to urban areas in search of rapidly vanishing industrial jobs but finding their expectations of greater opportunity and economic security dashed. Single-mother families and poverty were still characteristic of many black families, and they were largely either ignored by family scholars or theorized as culturally deviant. Thus, notable family changes and the critique of families emerged in tandem with an evolving economy, an undeniable contradiction between the ideology of equality and the reality of legalized racial and gender inequalities, and a vibrant social protest movement.

Within this context, family scholars began to rethink narrow, culturally biased family theories; explore the significance of gender in family life; and revise prevailing theories that denied the viability of racial and ethnic minority families. Many of these changes in family studies were inspired by the feminist and civil rights movements, both of which challenged essentialist (or biological) theories that upheld sexism and racism and the notion that breadwinner-homemaker families were inherently superior. The discovery of severe intergenerational poverty amid the economic affluence of the 1950s (Harrington 1962) shocked many Americans, led politicians to declare a "war on poverty," and resulted in a few more studies of social class inequality among American families. Although such studies were sparse and marginalized, research on African American families conducted prior to the 1960s typically embraced a social class perspective, perhaps because focusing on how economic factors shaped black families deflected attention from racist notions that black families were essentially alike and inherently inferior (Frazier [1939] 1957; Furstenberg 2007). A few other scholars also examined the impact of poverty and social class inequality. For example, in the early 1940s, Earl Lomon Koos (1946) conducted a case study of low-income families living in New York City that focused on the economic difficulties they encountered that made them feel inferior and insecure. Many of the couples Koos studied were foreign born and had come to the United States with the hope of finding a better life, but instead they were living in poverty and stigmatizing conditions. In another study, Richard Sennett (1973) examined how family life in a once-affluent Chicago neighborhood underwent significant changes as middle-class families were replaced by working-class families. Sennett noted sharp class divisions between families and resentment among the blue-collar workers because white-collar workers earned two to three times as much as skilled and unskilled workers (p. 84). Other research found differences in the way working- and middle-class families socialized their children, notably reproducing the social class structure (Kohn 1963), and provided an in-depth look at the struggles of working-class families by comparing them to middle-class families (Komarovsky 1962; Rubin 1976).

This book builds on this work by focusing on the impact of economic systems and social class on the organization of family life. Because the most vital function of the family is to ensure the survival of its members, I give primacy to the economic system in structuring the broad parameters of family life; that is, the economy shapes the prospects families have for earning a decent living by determining the location, nature, and pay associated with work. As discussed in more detail in Chapter 1, I do not assign families a passive role in this process, but rather argue that from early hunting and gathering societies to contemporary societies, the organization of family life is best understood in the context of economic forces. The power of economic forces to transform families is evident in the fact that most family scholars situate the study of Western families in the context of the industrial economy that began to emerge in the 1700s, noting how it gradually separated family life from work; fostered massive patterns of immigration and urbanization; led to modernization; created new specialized institutions and professions (e.g., psychology); and shaped marital, family, and gender ideologies. The rise of the industrial economy also resulted in the social class stratification that continues to exist in capitalist societies, initially polarizing capitalist owners and workers but then gradually giving rise to a multilevel class system that fostered socioeconomic mobility for many. That social class system continues to exist and has taken on new contours as the economy transitioned from industrial production to an information and services economy and became more globalized. This new post-industrial economy has been a major factor in drawing women into the labor force, creating greater class polarization and inequality, and influencing patterns of marriage and childbearing.

The intersection of economic and ideological forces in shaping families has been a major theme in family studies, and I hope to deepen that analysis by looking at family life in a broader historical and cultural context, exploring the emergence of institutionalized inequalities, and analyzing families in the context of social stratification theories. At the heart of this book, however, is an examination of the impact of social class on family life. I contend that, although most research implicitly focuses on middle-class families and a few studies more explicitly on poor families, social class analysis is rarely the major paradigm for studying the overall organization of and interpersonal relationships in families. Still, much research confirms that social class has a powerful impact on virtually every aspect of family life, such as whether and when one marries, how many children couples have and when, how children are socialized, and how gender is organized in families. I argue that although social inequalities based on gender, race, and ethnicity continue to exist and, obviously, affect families, social class position cuts across these dimensions of inequality in its ability to explain family life. The social class status of a family, for example, powerfully shapes its gender ideologies and relationships, and growing class diversity makes it impossible to theorize racial/ethnic minority families as monolithic entities. Thus, this book recognizes and explores how the broader economy shapes family life and examines the organization of family life across the social class hierarchy.

This Introduction is devoted to providing the broader theoretical framework of the book. I offer a perspective for understanding families that shifts the lens from seeing the family as an exclusively ideological or sentimental entity to a sociological perspective that understands families as economic and political entities. When families are examined within this framework, it becomes evident that dominant definitions of families and the nature of family life are shaped by power relations and thus subject to negotiation, debate, and resistance. Contemporary debates, such as those that focus on how to define a family, whether and/or why the family is declining, and the consequences of family transitions, are deeply rooted in history. In this Introduction, I briefly discuss historical debates over the family and how they have been tied to social unrest and protest, a resurgence of which was evident during the 1960s and 1970s. Protests during this era focused primarily on depictions of and theories about racial and ethnic minority families and issues of gender inequality, although some attention was devoted to social class inequality. I end this Introduction by defining the concept of social class, discussing its origins and relevance for understanding families, and providing an overview of the book.

Understanding Families in Social Context

I enjoy asking my students what images come to mind when they think about the word *family* because their answers always reveal the profoundly ideological nature of families. For example, students routinely offer words like security, love, acceptance, and stability in their descriptions of the family. Many students—although fewer than in the past—also express their concern over the decline in families, which they define largely in terms of fragile marriages, high rates of divorce, the number of children born to single parents, and sometimes the issue of marital rights for same-sex couples. Understanding the ideological nature of families is important because it highlights the sentimental value we place on families and speaks to the saliency of families in our lives. Indeed, families are often described in sociology as *primary institutions* because they have such an early and pivotal influence in our lives, and our concern over their viability reflects our need for human relationships that foster our growth and stand the test of time. Nevertheless, the ideological perspective is limited when it comes to understanding how families come to be organized in certain ways and why they change over time. Thinking of families solely in ideological terms typically privileges one family structure (e.g., heterosexual, married couples with children) over others; views family change as threatening; and attributes change to the behaviors of individuals or specific groups or people, who are then criticized for ignoring or undermining important family values. For example, from an ideological perspective, one might conclude that family change is related to a decline in moral or religious values or a general disregard for time-honored traditions that have sustained societies for centuries.

Ideologies do, of course, matter, and they may persist in shaping families even when they no longer make sense from an economic standpoint. For example, the ideology of individualism has deep roots in Western culture and has historically shaped family life. Individualism arguably accounts for the fact that Europeans historically have been less likely than people on other continents to organize family systems around extended kin systems (or clans) or accept that marriages should be arranged or mandatory and more likely to endorse independent singlehood and monogamous marriages (Goldthorpe 1987:5–6). Goldthorpe posits that Christianity was the major ideological force resulting in individualism because it taught that marriages should be monogamous, held that valid marriages had to be based on mutual consent, and forbade remarriages. But underlying individualism are economic forces that made the ideology feasible, such as the creation of the market economy in the Western world. Traced to its earliest origins, the family was a survival strategy that helped people deal with economic scarcity (Cherlin 2008:510). When survival was no longer an issue for the majority of people, as was increasingly the case in the Western world, new ideologies about families and marriages began to emerge. For example, by the sixteenth century, many Europeans were starting to view marriage as optional and argue that it should be based on romantic love and free choice. People increasingly had the resources to live outside the boundaries of marriage, and because singlehood was acceptable, many did so. But those who did marry held higher expectations of marriage, envisioning it as a source of companionship and emotional fulfillment. Sociologist Andrew Cherlin (2008) argues that many of the changes in marriage and family life throughout the twentieth century can be seen as an acceleration of individualism; from an economic perspective, people are less reliant on marriage for survival and less likely to subordinate their own needs and identities to traditions.

Because the primary function of families is survival, strategies and practices that contributed to the survival of families (e.g., the gender-based division of labor) often became the basis for ideologies that were endowed with moral or religious significance or encoded into laws. Thus, families are also political entities, in the sense that they are the result of laws that have been negotiated and passed that govern marriage and various aspects of family life. The state defines what constitutes a family, creates laws that specify who can marry, and defines the rights and responsibilities of married people as spouses, parents, and property owners (Goodsell 1934; Weitzman 1981). Thus, families and marriages are subject to power relations; more specifically, they tend to reflect the interests of dominant groups and social institutions and are often contested and negotiated by competing factions. The effort in Europe to make marriage a sacrament of the church, for example, was a matter of much debate, and ambiguity over what constituted a legal marriage continued through the nineteenth century (Thornton, Axinn, and Xie 2007).

Laws about marriage and family life are often based on economic forces, and they typically reflect the interests of privileged groups (e.g., economically prosperous white men); thus, they create social inequalities that often result in social unrest. Yet, once they are institutionalized and ideologically justified, they are often resistant to change. In the past, laws protected the economic position of slave owners by defining enslaved Africans as property rather than human beings, banning them from entering legalized marriages, and allowing their family members to be separated and sold. With the rise of industry, slavery became less profitable and more contested and was eventually abolished, yet the ideology of black inferiority was used to justify segregation and govern race relations for another century. Similarly, exploiting the labor and resources of other racial groups, such as Native Americans, was often justified by the argument that they were less civilized than white people. The domination of women by men rested on patriarchal ideologies that have an even longer history than the concept of race, and it was upheld by laws that defined women as having a subordinate status in families and the public arena, legitimized male domination, and denied women basic citizenship rights. Not surprisingly, social inequality has often led to social protest.

Social Inequality: The Seeds of Discontent

The perspective that I embrace in this book gives primacy to economic forces and argues that they are typically the basis for political and ideological forces that define and shape families. Because dominant groups control these forces in ways that reflect their own economic interests, they often create social inequalities that ignite social protest, unrest, and even warfare among competing groups. Indeed, social protest has been common throughout American history, often sparked during economic transitions. From the 1600s through the early 1900s, the promise of economic opportunity drew millions of immigrants to the New World—the United States—but rather than the open system of mobility and opportunity that they expected, many encountered racial and ethnic discrimination, economic exploitation, and dire living conditions. Such treatment was often motivated by economic and political fears, along with ethnocentric beliefs in English superiority. The early English immigrants not only controlled the economy and the political arena, they held a host of negative stereotypes about white ethnic groups who were from the southern and eastern regions of Europe (e.g., Italians, Poles, Jews). On the one hand, they welcomed them as laborers, but they were fearful of allowing "weak and ignorant" immigrants to participate in the political system. Thus, despite images of the United States as a classless society and even a melting pot, white ethnic groups were subjected to assimilation processes such as Americanization campaigns in which they pledged allegiance and conformity to the dominant WASP culture (Kivisto 2002).

People of color faced an even harsher system of racial stratification that disrupted their family and cultural traditions, resulted in a massive loss of their land and resources, and relegated them to the lowest-paying jobs in the labor market. Unlike white ethnics, who were expected to assimilate into the dominant society, racial minorities experienced various forms of coercive pluralism (Fuchs 1990:8–6). According to Fuchs, Native Americans encountered a form of *predatory pluralism*: They were displaced from their own land; defined as uncivilized; and subjected to contagious diseases, military campaigns, and genocide. Mexicans faced a similar fate: Through war and negotiation, much of what had been Mexico was incorporated into the United States, and Mexicans became foreigners and temporary labor migrants on territory they once owned. The thousands of Chinese who immigrated to the United States to escape the political and economic upheaval in China and participate in the gold rush in the western region of the nation also found themselves relegated to a secondary status (Glenn 1983). Chinese immigrants were mostly male and frequently subjected to economic exclusion, mob violence, segregation, discriminatory laws, and stereotypes. Fuchs (1990) characterizes the experiences of Mexicans and Chinese as *sojourner pluralism,* as the majority came to work and support the families they left behind, with the dream of eventually returning to their families. Finally, African Americans confronted a form of *caste pluralism* because they were concentrated at the bottom of the national economy, politically disenfranchised, and socially stigmatized. Fuchs explains that the abolition of slavery, which had been instituted by the seventeenth century and lasted for more than 250 years, did not end the racial caste system; rather, it endured until the middle of the twentieth century.

Resistance to social inequalities has been endemic and spanned centuries. Warfare between native populations and white Europeans over land, labor, and resources; inter-ethnic conflict over jobs; slave rebellions; violent confrontations between workers and their employers; and struggles by women for equal rights have characterized American society from its origins through the early decades of the twentieth century (H. Zinn [1980] 2003). Civil unrest and social protest shaped American society, in some cases presenting effective challenges to engrained patterns of social inequality. For example, the exclusion of women from the industrial labor force in the 1800s and the creation of the breadwinner-homemaker family coincided with the rise of the nineteenth-century feminist movement. This early feminist protest movement was led primarily by middle-class white women and was eventually successful in reaching its goals of opening educational opportunities for women, securing full political rights, and gaining property rights and legal personhood for women (Goodsell 1934:466). Slavery was abolished partially in response to the demise of the agricultural economy, but also as a result of efforts by abolitionists to end the economic and social degradation of African Americans. Although racial segregation was soon to follow slavery as the law of the land, by the early twentieth century, African Americans were moving from the southern sharecropping system to industrial and domestic jobs in the north. But the post-World War II economic affluence of the United States, and of the many wage and benefit concessions organized labor gained from employers, led to a decline in ethnic conflict over jobs. By the 1950s, the majority of white ethnic groups had been fully assimilated into mainstream society (Kivisto 2002), often holding jobs in the industrial economy that enabled them to realize the American Dream of a middle-class lifestyle.

The Revolutions of the 1960s and 1970s

The peace and prosperity that characterized the 1950s once led scholars to call the era "the golden age of the family," yet beneath the façade of happy, middle-class families a confluence of ideological, economic, and political forces were already sowing the seeds of discontent. One lingering issue was that racial segregation, which had been used in propaganda during World War II to tarnish the image of the United States as defenders of liberty, was still upheld by laws. The use of racist ideologies in Europe to justify genocide and atrocities against Jews during the war provided fertile ground for questioning the concept of race, including biological theories of race. Thus, the end of World War II ushered in an especially propitious time for rethinking longstanding racial inequalities. In a notable book titled *An American Dilemma*, Gunnar Myrdal (1944) exposed the contradiction between the ideology of equality and the oppression of African Americans. Although they clearly had not transcended racist thinking and theorizing, many social scientists had already begun to conceptualize race as more a social than a biological construct and to argue that the social environment, rather than genes, shapes behaviors and families.

Latent racism continued to characterize the field of family studies. The dominant trend was to portray white families as superior and as middle-class entities and to accept, sometimes quite explicitly, that black families were inferior, pathological, and excluded from the American Dream (Truxal and Merrill 1947). Countering that trend was the use of a social class perspective among the handful of scholars studying African American families as shaped by social environmental and cultural factors (S. Hill 2005; Furstenberg 2007). These scholars held that the legacy of slavery, northward migration, and persistent racism were the major factors responsible for the hardships that African Americans encountered but argued that, among the middle class, black and white families were quite similar (Davis and Havighurst 1946). Still, these researchers described poor, single-mother families in dire and stereotypical ways—a strategy probably meant as a call for government intervention, but later seen as proffering a social deficit perspective on black families that blamed them for their own poverty and disadvantage.

Meanwhile, it was evident that there was gap between the ideology of the happy housewife and the lived experiences of many white, middle-class women. Betty Friedan (1963) captured widespread discontent among white, middle-class housewives in *The Feminine Mystique,* a book often credited with igniting the second wave of feminism. Friedan argued that many housewives were experiencing the "problem without a name"; that is, they had a feeling of malaise and emotional emptiness that was marked by myriad physical and psychological symptoms. Moreover, due to their dissatisfaction with the housewife role and the changing economy, many were entering (or reentering) the labor market. The industrial economy was, in fact, already in transition by the mid-twentieth century, with manufacturing jobs in decline and information and services jobs, which were often seen as jobs for women, increasing. Friedan's book advanced a liberal feminism that supported the rights of women to fulfill their potential by entering the public arena on an equal footing with men.

This intersection of ideological and economic forces ignited the social protest movements of the 1960s, specifically the feminist and civil rights movements. Feminists argued that "sex roles"—the study of which had come to dominate research on modern families—were far from merely a functional, benign strategy for dividing family work in an equitable fashion. Rather, the notion of sex roles was based on flawed biological reasoning that saw one's abilities as a product of innate traits (e.g., women as nurturing, men as aggressive) and upheld the notion of female inferiority. Feminists made a crucial distinction between biological sex and gender, contending that the latter was socially constructed. Gender expectations shaped personal identity but, more broadly, reinforced a system of gender stratification that disadvantaged women in virtually every area of life; thus, the family was criticized as a central arena for perpetuating gendered relations. At the core of the breadwinner-homemaker family was a sexist ideology that made women dependent on marriage and men for their survival and kept many wives in unsatisfying and even abusive relationships. Feminists questioned the notion that women were somehow naturally suited for the housewife-mother role, or that they should have to choose between family and career, and explored the consequences of patriarchal families. For some, the family was recast as a major system of female oppression because it was organized on the basis of gender and socialized children into accepting the gender order (Risman 1998). This reemergence of feminism in the twentieth century helped catapult families to the center of contention over gender inequality; moreover, its critique resonated with that of revisionist scholars who were rethinking earlier depictions of African American families.

Civil rights activists called into question the dominant theoretical discourse in the field of family studies, namely that racial minority families were inherently dysfunctional if they failed to conform to the breadwinner-homemaker family structure. Their political stance especially took issue with the suggestion that single-mother families, rather than racism and segregation, were responsible for the plight of African Americans. Focusing on the stigmatizing and stereotypical depictions of African Americans in poor families, a new cadre of scholars argued that research on black families had utilized a social deficit perspective that portrayed black families as pathological. In response, scholars shifted their focus to a cultural perspective, emphasizing the way African Americans had drawn on cultural resources to create strong families despite racial oppression. Based on this perspective, cultural traditions such as the extended family, flexible gender roles, shared childrearing, and dual-income families were among the strengths of African American families (R. Hill 1972). The cultural perspective reshaped theorizing about black families by placing them in a more favorable light and helped counter the tendency to blame them for their own disadvantaged status. The potency of the cultural perspective, however, waned as economic transitions, social policies, and greater class diversity among African Americans emerged (see Chapter 2).

The social protest movements of the 1960s and 1970s sparked a broader human liberation that included other marginalized groups, such as the elderly, gays and lesbians, and the disabled, and helped transform the field of family studies. Family scholars began to debate the universality and merits of families, and longstanding family ideologies were questioned and often cast aside. No longer do family scholars accept the notion that the breadwinner-homemaker family model is the norm for most families or the only viable structure for those that function well, and there is more research on dual-income families and family diversity. Most researchers recognize gender is a major structure that impacts virtually every aspect of family life; rarely does a family textbook fail to include a chapter or substantial attention to the many dimensions of gender (e.g., gendered violence, gender socialization, the gender division of housework). In fact, gender is often the central paradigm used in research and studies of families (see, e.g., Leeder 2004; S. Hill 2005; Coltrane and Adams 2008). In her decade review of research on gender in family studies, Myra Marx Ferree (2010) noted substantial progress in the focus on gender relations in families, but cites as central weaknesses the persistent tendency to cast certain families (e.g., same-sex, female-headed) as deviant and the failure to explore families in the broader context of political and economic changes. Much more attention is devoted to understanding how race and ethnicity affect family life, and such families are no longer seen as inherently inferior or dysfunctional (B. Dickerson 1995; McAdoo 1998; Dunaway 2003). Studies have become more inclusive of the lives and relationships of same-sex couples and have devoted more attention to studying aging families and intergenerational relationships (Savin-Williams and Esterberg 2000; Rosenfeld 2007).

Protest over racial and gender inequalities has led to significant economic, occupational, and educational gains for racial minorities and women. Laws have declared discrimination based on factors such as religion, nationality, race, and gender to be illegal, and many schools and employers have taken measures to diversify their populations and workforces. While still underrepresented in many settings, women and racial minorities have made significant gains. In 1960, women received only 35 percent of the bachelor's degrees awarded, but they received 58 percent of those awarded in 2004 (Buchmann and DiPrete 2006). Women are now just as likely as men to attend law and medical schools (Gilbert 2008) and have proven to be viable candidates for the highest political offices in the country. Although the wages of women as a group still lag behind those of men, the gender gap in wages has nearly closed among young, college-educated men and women. Strides toward gender equality have also been made in the private arena of home, with men and women much more likely today to share responsibility for housework and child care (Sullivan 2006).

Wage, wealth, and educational gaps still exist between whites and racial minority groups, yet the overall picture is one of significant gains by racial minorities. In 1940, African Americans graduated from high school at a rate just one-third that of their white counterparts—14 percent compared to 46 percent—and an estimated 80 percent of black people occupied the three lowest-paid occupational categories. The racial gap in high school attainment was nearly closed by 1970, and by 2002, 25 percent of African Americans had managerial/professional positions and another 25 percent had white-collar sales and clerical jobs (Gilbert 2008). Similarly, prior to the civil rights movement, the majority of Asian American workers, regardless of their skills or level of educational attainment, were found in low-paying marginalized jobs. Since that time, however, they have made remarkable occupational gains (Sakamoto, Goyette, and Kim 2009), with Asian American households now earning higher wages than white households. Other racial minorities have not fared as well, however; in fact, a recent review found that white families still earn strikingly more than Hispanic, African American, and Native American families (Burton et al. 2010). The rate of poverty among African Americans, for example, is nearly 25 percent—but still significantly less than the 60 percent rate that existed prior to the 1960s.

Despite this progress, neither racial nor gender equality has been achieved. One reason is that economic inequality has sharpened, and progress made by racial minorities and women has fallen along social class lines. Feminist theorists have argued that race, class, and gender are intersecting dimensions of social inequality, yet the focus on race and gender often obscures the reality of social class divisions. For example, from its origins the women's movement was criticized for its emphasis on issues that primarily pertained to the lives of white middle-class women. Many racial/ethnic minority women eschewed the white feminist notion of motherhood as oppressive and, living with economic marginality and the struggle to balance paid and family work, failed to understand how male wage-earner families were problematic. These differences were often interpreted as the result of different cultures, especially given the rising prominence of the cultural perspective in black family studies, but more often reflected economic differences between women. The cultural perspective on black families tended to focus on life strategies among the poor and generalize them to all African American families, inadvertently creating a monolithic image of black families. Yet throughout the twentieth century, social class differences among African Americans grew as the occupational structure changed and opportunities increased, making it nearly impossible to say anything about the mythical "black family."

Making Social Class Visible

This book foregrounds the impact of social class on family life. Social class has become one of the best-developed areas of sociology, although it was slow to develop in the United States. Because the nation lacked a rigid social class system, such as the one that existed in Europe for centuries, and endorsed creeds of democracy, equal opportunity, and upward mobility, the founders of American sociology held a relatively classless view of society (Kerbo 2009). When they did turn their attention to social class stratification, their work was shaped by widespread concern over the spread of communism, and many idealized the American family as being proof of the success of capitalism (May 1999). Thus, their study of social class stratification eschewed notions of class conflict and exploitation; theorized class stratification as natural and essential to the social order (see Chapter 3); and focused on factors such as prestige, power, status, and social mobility. For example, in the 1930s, Lloyd Warner (1949) set out to study social class in a New England city but concluded that distinctions based on status were more important than those based on class. Another seminal study focused on the issue of status attainment and delineated those factors that were responsible for social mobility among Americans (Blau and Duncan 1967).

Although a critical perspective on social class was being embraced by the 1960s, with social class shown to be one of the strongest predictors of behaviors and attitudes, a consistent concern among scholars has been that social class awareness in the United States has remained marginal. The reality of social class divisions is often obscured by the fact that the United States is a wealthy nation, widespread depictions of America as a middle-class nation, the ideology of the American Dream, and the belief in upward class mobility through hard work and determination. Diminished social class awareness is also fostered by the fact that the mention of economic inequality, especially when mentioned by politicians, is often interpreted as an effort to incite "class warfare" (Perrucci and Wysong 2008). The argument that social class awareness among Americans is marginal does not mean they do not understand that there are wealthy, middle-class, and poor people, but rather that few grasp the antagonistic relationship between the classes, understand the role of exploitation of workers by employers as important, or view social inequality as unfair or a permanent feature of life. The importance of social factors, such as poor schools, labor policies, and discrimination, in perpetuating class inequality is often ignored. Racial politics also deflect attention from social class. Historically, white people have been more interested in color than class, and this often meant that poor and working-class whites often paid more attention to distancing themselves from racial minorities than focusing on their own class disadvantages (Bowser 2007). Stories of people who rose from their humble origins to wealth and success through their own individual attributes, such as having a strong work ethic and seeking an education, have been more salient.

In recent decades, however, social class inequality has risen substantially and has become more apparent. Since the 1970s, there has been a decline in the industrial sector of the economy, a weakening of the power of organized labor and its ability to defend the wages and benefits of workers, a more globalized system of labor, and the enactment of legislation that has benefited the wealthy at the expense of others. The rise of the post-industrial economy has been pivotal in growing social class polarization in the United States; it initially resulted in the loss of millions of highly paid manufacturing jobs, and gradually, in the context of the global economy, it began to erode the pay and benefits of white-collar workers. Perrucci and Wysong (2008:29–30) document the massive job loss that has occurred in recent decades, the increasing use of low-paid contingency workers who lack employer-provided benefits such as health care, and a greater tendency for Americans to experience downward mobility. To illustrate the growing rate of class polarization and the demise of the middle class, they proffer a new double-diamond class structure that places 20 percent of the population in the privileged class and the other 80 percent in the new working class. The major factors dividing the two groups are access to life-sustaining resources such as investment and social capital and the stability of those resources over time.

The results of growing economic disadvantage have been more concern among Americans over job security and greater social class awareness. Surveys show that most people now believe that losing their jobs is a real possibility, and many who have always seen themselves as middle class are having more difficulty making ends meet. Thus, they are becoming more critical of class inequality and more favorable toward governmental intervention. One study describes Americans as "conservative egalitarians"; that is, they support a blend of philosophical conservatism (e.g., belief in free enterprise and individual responsibility) with an operational liberalism, a belief that the government should intervene and help address barriers to opportunity (Page and Jacobs 2009).

Defining Social Class

The concept of social class is associated with the rise of market economies and the industrial economy and refers to the fact that people occupy different positions in a multilevel economy (Wright 2008). The analysis of social class inequality originated with the work of Karl Marx and Frederic Engels (Hout 2008), who were nineteenth-century critics of industrial capitalism and its exploitation of workers. Marx and Engels contended that the industrial revolution had produced only two historically significant social classes: capitalists, who owned the means of production, and workers, who were being exploited by working long hours for low pay in abysmal working conditions. Another nineteenth-century social theorist, Max Weber, broadened the Marxist concept of social class. Weber argued that one's social class was based on several factors, namely income, prestige, and power, and that social class position determined one's life chances, or the opportunity people had to lead successful and gratifying lives. Most definitions of social class in the United States reflect the Weberian influence. For example, social classes have been defined as "groups of families more or less equal in rank and differentiated from other families above or below them with regard to characteristics such as occupation, income, wealth, and prestige" (Gilbert 2008:11).

Social class and socioeconomic status are used interchangeably by most scholars, but there is a slight distinction between the two concepts. *Social class* captures the more Marxist perspective as it refers to one's position in the industrial labor market and emphasizes the exploitation of workers by business owners and managers (Wright 2008). *Socioeconomic status* is more in line with the work of Weber and is defined by multiple variables. The Hollingshead Two-Factor Index of Social Position, designed to measure socioeconomic status and widely used by researchers, reflects the Weberian perspective. It ranks a person's occupation and education on a scale from one to seven to determine his or her social class position (note that income is not explicitly included). This is the most widely used scale of socioeconomic class in sociology, although scholars often use, singly or collectively, education, income, and occupation as measures of social class.

Although social class is one of the core areas of sociological investigation and—arguably—the best-developed area in the discipline, it is also a dynamic and contentious area of study. The divide between Marxist and Weberian scholars remains, although the former (neo-Marxist) have often revised and broadened some of the basic precepts of Marxist theory to deal with the complexities of the current labor market. The scope of the field of study also presents challenges. Wright (2008:330), a neo-Marxist scholar, defines the study of social class as including the distribution of material resources, how classes have changed historically, how people subjectively place themselves in the social class structure, life chances, and the more Marxist concepts of class antagonism, conflict, and emancipatory ideals.

Combining the legacies of Marx and Weber, Gilbert (2008:10–11) identifies 10 variables that are included in the study of social class stratification: occupation, wealth, income, poverty, prestige, socialization, association, social mobility, power, and class consciousness.

The analysis of social class had become a major field of sociological inquiry by the 1920s, with theorists focusing largely on identifying how many social classes existed, how to measure social class, and the process of class formation in the United States. Although Marx and Engels argued for a two-tier class structure of owners and workers, most twentieth-century Marxists saw the limitations of that model and sought to broaden it. Depictions of the social class structure are, in fact, ideal types or analytical categories that help explain social phenomena; thus, social scientists have developed schemes ranging from two to six social classes. Still, the boundaries separating social classes are not always clear and distinct. Since socioeconomic status is based on multiple factors, class inconsistencies and ambiguities occur. For example, it is difficult to define the social class position of a high school dropout who wins the lottery and instantly becomes a millionaire. Based on income, she might be in the upper class, yet in all probability she would lack the educational and cultural resources and social capital that marks the lifestyles of people in that class.

Despite these difficulties, scholars have consistently found that social class has a major impact on individuals and families. For example, in the earliest study of social class formation, Robert and Helen Lynd conducted a longitudinal study of the rise of social class stratification between 1890 and 1935 in a typical American city as it underwent the transition from agricultural and small market economy to machine production (Gilbert 2003:46–47). They documented the progressive polarization of the community into a large working class and a smaller business class and argued that birth of either side of this cleavage influenced virtually every aspect of life—marital choices, religion, political participation, and so on (pp. 46–47). In later work, these authors developed a schema that included six different social classes, but they maintained that the "business folk" in the top three tiers (the upper, upper middle, and lower middle classes) consistently worked together to thwart the interests of those in the bottom three classes (the upper working class, lower working class, and marginal class; pp. 51–50).

This work understands families as integral to the social stratification system; they perpetuate social class stratification through their social structural locations and lifestyles, practices of racial and class homogamy in marriage, patterns of child socialization, and transmission of wealth (Elmelech 2008). Thus, this book explores families in social class perspective.

Brief Overview of Chapters

In Chapter 1, I show how family systems and ideologies are intertwined with and shaped by economic forces. I point out that it is nearly impossible to trace the origins of the family because it evolved primarily as a strategy for ensuring survival. Still, as family studies evolved in the mid-nineteenth century, scholars often debated the origins of the family, many inspired more by their religious and political ideologies than empirical evidence (Lamanna 2002). What is evident is that families and ideologies about families have evolved with economic systems, fostering specific marriage systems and notions about the roles of men and women. Most evident was the transformation of families that resulted from the advent of the market economy and industrialization, which fostered the separation of work and family, the ideology of separate spheres for women and men, and, at least initially, higher rates of family instability. Although early scholars often saw industrialization as resulting in the decline of families, by the turn of the twentieth century, most heralded the superiority of the modern nuclear family for rearing children, meeting the emotional and sexual needs of adults, and fostering social mobility. I show how the concepts of family and marriage are socially constructed, typically by dominant groups and in ways that can be used to exploit women and racial and ethnic minority groups. As capitalist markets expanded, family ideologies were also used to dominate and marginalize people across the globe. Through international exploration and trade, white Europeans were able to establish their economic, political, and family systems as superior while characterizing others as primitive, deficient, and even non-human.

Chapter 2 looks at how classical and contemporary sociologists have theorized social inequality. Two major theories—structural functionalism and conflict theory—are typically seen as polar opposites in their approach to social inequality and their family ideologies, and both are discussed in this chapter. Symbolic interactionism, not typically seen as a theory of social inequality, is also addressed because it was widely utilized in the study of families and provides key insights into understanding how status and social class are socially defined. Symbolic interactionism also has provided the basis for understanding how race and gender inequality emerges, and theories of these inequalities are also included.

Chapters 3 to 5 are devoted to looking at family life among wealthy or upper-class families, middle-income families, and low-income or poor families. Each chapter starts with a definition of that class and brief history of its origin and covers its patterns of marriage, fertility, and childbearing. Beyond that, the chapters focus on issues that especially pertain to each social class.

For example, the chapter on middle-class families includes a discussion of the changing economy and its impact on their economic status, and the chapter on economically marginal families looks at poverty and social policies.

Finally, Chapter 6 explores the challenges brought to families as economies globalized. The expansion of capitalism to new markets across the world sparked a (sometimes painful) process of modernization, and the advent of new technologies created a global economy that was impossible to ignore. We became more aware than ever before that the fate of families is intricately linked to the economy; for example, the new economy offered a proliferation of female-typed jobs and led to a demise of the male provider role—not just in the United States but globally. Lower rates of marriage and higher rates of singlehood, nonmarital childbearing, and family instability are global phenomena.

For my husband, Edwin C. Hill, Sr.

1

The Evolution of
Families and Marriages

F amilies are essentially care institutions that vary across cultures and
change over time. Their essential function, historically, has been to
contribute to the basic economic survival of family members; thus, the structure of families often adapts to the economy, and cultural ideologies and
laws are created to reinforce that adaptation. Over time, societies grow and
become more complex and stratified, and the nature and quality of life
among families becomes differentiated based on varying economies and the
particular position of the family within the economic system. Broadly speaking, social scientists have identified four major economies that have existed
across the span of human history: hunting and gathering (or foraging),
agrarian/agricultural, modern/industrial, and service/knowledge-based economies. All these economies still exist in various parts of the world, and
nations often have mixed economies. Families of some sort existed and
continue to exist in all of these economies and, as social institutions, are
perhaps as old as humankind. Marriage, on the other hand, is a more recent
institution. Because hunting and gathering societies existed for millennia, it
is quite likely that some form of marriage, or at least temporary partnering
between women and men, emerged in the early versions of these societies. In
foraging societies, however, marriage as a stable partnership between men
and women probably took a backseat to family ties. Indeed, it was membership in the family that best ensured physical and economic survival.

This chapter has several purposes. The first is to briefly define the family
and marriage, discuss their origins, and explain how they evolved in tandem

with economic development. In this book, I foreground economic forces as transforming families and ultimately shaping the nature and quality of family life, as a prelude to chapters that look at families from a social class perspective. However, it is important to keep in mind that, as pointed out above, other social structural forces (e.g., ideologies, politics) also shape families. Thus, there is no rigid, universal, or inevitable link between family structure, economy, and ideology; instead, people are active, cognitive beings who may respond to structural forces in a variety of ways (Jayakody, Thornton, and Axinn 2008). In fact, as social institutions, the family and economy are mutually interactive and influential, so families may also shape aspects of the economy. As historian Tamara Hareven (1991) explains, families are not separate entities but are intricately connected to other social institutions, such as religion and work; thus, they do not merely react to economic and ideological changes, but they can initiate or resist such changes (p. 96). Families may mediate the demands of the economy by deciding which family members will be involved in productive labor or by embracing values that emphasize achievement and success (Furstenberg 1966).

This chapter also explores the early origins of the major types of social inequality discussed in this book—inequalities based on social class, race/ethnicity, and gender. Scholars agree that although some forms of social inequality probably existed in the earliest societies, perhaps based on the differing talents and abilities of people, such inequalities were not particularly rigid or consequential. People in early foraging societies were often nomadic and lacked surplus wealth or even the concept of property ownership, and thus they had little basis for creating a significant stratification system. The emergence of settled societies, however, was marked by the discovery of agriculture and the domestication of animals and fostered the rise of institutionalized inequalities based on social class, ethnicity, race, and gender. These social inequalities reflect differences in economic development, wealth, and power, and, as societies advance, they are rationalized based on religious teachings, ethnocentric attitudes, and cultural ideologies.

The emergence and expansion of capitalist markets in Europe during the 1500s offers one example of the interaction between economic and ideological forces and the impact they can have on notions of family. The growth of capitalism during this era led to an expansion of wealth, the growth of the middle class, and the rise of Enlightenment thinkers who challenged the power of monarchs and championed the virtues of the free market, individualism, freedom, and human rights. These ideals also led to new thinking about marriage, such as the contention that it should be based on free choice and romantic love. Although Enlightenment ideals were rarely expanded to include equality for women, they did arguably elevate the status of women by suggesting that marriages should be entered into by mutual consent and that women were partners in marriage rather than a form of property.

Such ideals influenced the Europeans who migrated to the New World to expand the British Empire. The chapter concludes by looking at the gender and racial order they created in the New World and how the transition from an agricultural to an industrial economy affected families. During the early decades of the twentieth century, America struggled to create breadwinner-homemaker families and, by the mid-1940s, had succeeded in promoting itself as a middle class society. Such illusion, however, proved short-lived, and by the 1970s social inequality was again on the national agenda. In the ensuing decades, social class inequality among Americans spiraled, creating a pattern of social class polarization that included greater wealth for the wealthy, deeper poverty and economic hardship for the working class and poor, and a notable decline in the middle class.

Families and Marriage: A Brief History

Sociologists understand families to be social institutions that perform vital functions for their members and societies: They produce, nurture, and social-ize children; care for frail and elderly family members; provide the laborers needed for the economy; and meet the emotional needs of family members. To describe families as social entities recognizes the fact that they are socially created and defined and vary across cultures; to refer to them as institutions means that they embody a set of interrelated roles and responsibilities. Cross-cultural differences, the changing nature of families, and political forces often have made defining the family a matter of some contention. By the mid-twentieth century, social scientists had developed definitions of the family that seemed broadly inclusive in terms of capturing the essence of family life across cultures. For example, one family scholar defined the fam-ily based on its structure, functions, and attributes, noting that

> [The family] consists of husband, wife, and children born in their wedlock, though other relatives may find their place close to this nuclear group; and the group is united by moral, legal, economic, religious, and social rights and obligations (including sexual rights and prohibitions as well as such socially patterned feelings as love, attraction, piety, and awe). (Coser [1964] 2004:13)

But even seemingly broad definitions of the family such as this are contested by scholars who point out that families are not always based on heterosexu-ality and marriage and do not always include children, nuclear households, romantic love, or consensual sexual relations (Gittins 1993).

The Concept of Marriage

Empirical evidence on the origins of marriage is scant, as it evolved cross-culturally at different times and has been defined in various ways. There is considerable agreement that as an institution, marriage is not as old as families. Whether the earliest societies had monogamous or polygamous marriages, practiced sexual restraint or sexual freedom, or were ruled by women (matriarchal) or men (patriarchal) were once issues that were much debated among social scientists, although those debates produced social theories that were based more on ideology than empirical facts (Lamanna 2002:41). For example, Friedrich Engels, a nineteenth-century social critic of capitalistic economies and patriarchal families, argued that maternal families existed in early primitive societies, where property was held communally, sexual relations were casual, and the family, when it was distinct from the larger group, was defined as mothers and their children (Adams and Steinmetz 1993). Cross-cultural studies offer numerous examples of cultures that have maternal families, although it bears noting that maternal families (in which mother-child relations and female-centered kin units are central, and fathers are more marginal) were not usually matriarchal families or families in which women held most of the power (Reuter and Runner 1931). Conversely, more religiously based theories held that male-dominated, monogamous marriages were God-ordained and had always existed. For many, such issues were important in understanding family change; however, by the mid-1900s most had abandoned such debates in favor of research on the new family system that was emerging as a result of the industrial economy (Lasch 1977).

The definition of marriage is less contested than its history: Marriage has almost universally been defined as a social and legal union between men and women, although a few cultures have allowed people of the same sex to marry (Coontz 2005). Sociologist Max Weber defined marriage as a "stable sexual relationship" allowed and legitimized by the larger kin group and used to determine rules about property rights for children (R. Collins 1986:276). The majority of marriages are based on monogamy—a union between one woman and one man—but many societies also have allowed people to have more than one spouse, or polygamous marriages. The Talmud, which comprises Jewish religious law and customs, allows men to have as many as four wives. Whether monogamous or polygamous, marriage systems do not emerge in a vacuum but, like families, are social institutions that serve a purpose. Thus, the practice of polygyny (or multiple wives) was often a strategy for increasing the population size, ensuring the production of male heirs or ensuring that all women in the society were taken care of when men were in short supply. Similarly, polyandry (or multiple husbands), though extremely rare, is associated with a shortage of women (sometimes due to female infanticide) and poverty. In this case, a young girl or woman may be betrothed to and shared by several brothers, thereby negating the need for them to divide meager resources or individually take on the role of supporting a wife.

Across cultures, the most universal feature of marriage has been gender division of labor between men and women (Coontz 2005; Buechler 2008). Almost everywhere, women's work has centered on activities that can be done at or near the home, such as gardening, gathering plants, weaving, pottery, and the care of small animals, while hunting, plowing, and herding cattle have typically been the work of men (R. Collins 1986). The fact that only women can give birth to and breastfeed children makes them the logical caregivers for children and is at the root of the gender division of family labor. Women's reproductive roles, however, historically did not exempt them from participating in economic labor, nor did they inherently lead to male domination. Although no cultures have been found that define women as the dominant group and nearly all subscribe at least ideologically to patriarchy, the degree of gender stratification across cultures ranges from near equality to extreme inequality. The integration of women into productive labor and kinship structures that emphasize blood ties over marital ties (Sanday 1981) and the ability of women to have children (Buechler 2008:193) often enhances their social status even when patriarchy is the cultural norm.

Early Hunting and Gathering Societies

Early foraging societies predated the discovery of agriculture. In such economies, small groups of nomadic people eked out a living as hunters and gatherers, often surviving at the subsistence level. Scarcity was often the norm, as were reciprocity and sharing. All members of the group—men, women, and children—were expected to contribute to the production of food. In subsistence economies, supporting nonproducers often threatened the survival of the group, and population size was kept small by means of abortion, infanticide, and sometimes even abandonment of the elderly.

Most scholars believe that a relative degree of social equality existed in foraging societies because most of them lacked surplus resources, the concept of private property, or the knowledge of biological paternity (Shlain 2003). Marriages or male-female partnering was likely informal, easily dissolved, and secondary to kinship ties, and there was little emphasis on female virginity, paternity, or lifelong unions, so there was no real incentive for men to dominate women (Coltrane and Adams 2008:54). Less nomadic hunting and gathering societies were sometimes matrilocal and allowed polyandry as a marital rule: Women could take several husbands, and the children retained the clan name of their mothers. Polyandrous marriage and matrilocal families were found in Hawaii and native populations in the Americas, Southeast Asia, and West Africa (Glassman, Swatos, and Denison 2004).

Until recent decades, it was common for social scientists studying families in cross-cultural context to use a developmental paradigm that saw all families as evolving from the simple, primitive entities that existed in foraging societies to the modern entities that emerged with industrialization (Lamanna 2002; Leeder 2004). Although this perspective still holds sway in some circles, the developmental paradigm is laden with ethnocentric assumptions because it contends that the diverse family forms found among non-Europeans are proof that they are spiritually or morally depraved (Thornton 2005). Moreover, the premise that the earliest economies, such as those based on hunting and gathering, are invariably evolving into modern economies is erroneous. Economies based mostly on hunting and gathering still exist today, with levels of technology and cultural practices that are diverse and have changed over time. Most are no longer nomadic, and they have gained considerable control over their environments and created complex political, social, and kinship systems. While scarcity is still often the norm, this has not precluded the development of stratification systems based on access to resources or status factors, such as being healers, hunters, chiefs, or religious leaders.

Settled Agricultural Societies: The Rise of Social Inequalities

Although inequalities were not unheard of in simple hunting and gathering societies, notable economic inequalities between people began to emerge 9,000–12,000 years ago in the Middle East when the cultivation of plants led to the development of agrarian economies based on farming and land ownership. For scholars, the creation of agrarian economies marked the advent of civilization, defined as settled societies that became increasingly complex (e.g., based on written rules and laws) and based on hierarchal relationships between people. Small-scale agrarian economies paved the way for larger agricultural economies, which turned plant cultivation and the domestication of animals into a major, and often scientific, enterprise. With such economies came the concept of personal ownership of labor and other natural resources, inheritance rights, the rise of serf and slave labor to plant and harvest crops, and the creation of political and economic laws to protect wealth (Rossides 1997:22–24).

Settled economies led to population growth, surplus production, and specialized occupations and institutions, all of which created the basis for a hierarchy among people based on wealth and status. Although the number of occupations increased, among those in agrarian and agricultural economies the most basic divisions are between two polarized groups: governing elites and peasants, landowners and the landless, or aristocratic/royal elites and the masses (Bowser 2007). Warfare and standing armies also emerged with agrarian and later large-scale agricultural economies, and they became significant for subordinating and stratifying populations. Social divisions between people in medieval Europe were often reflected in estate systems of stratification, with warfare the most important form of social power and one's legal status, rights, and privileges derived from family of birth.

Transformations in Families and Marriages

Families were gradually reshaped by the discovery of agriculture; for example, the right to own land and pass it on to heirs meant that women's child-bearing abilities and male domination became more important. Rather than kinship, marriage became the center of family life and was increasingly based on a formal contractual relationship between men, women, and their kinship groups. The property and gender implications of marriage are evident in the exchange of gifts between spouses and families and clearly defined rules about the rights and responsibilities of each marital partner. During the Middle Ages, economic factors influenced marital choices more than affection, even among the poor, and women's sexuality was treated as a form of property (Coltrane and Adams 2008:54). Wealth and power inequalities meant that marriages among the elite and/or governing classes were based largely on creating political alliances and producing male children (Coontz 2005). Ensuring paternity became important in the transfer of property to legitimate heirs, and the rights and sexuality of women were circumscribed. Ideologies of male domination prevailed, and women, especially those who were married to powerful men, were typically treated like chattel and given very few rights.

The property-like status of women was evident in Western societies like Rome and Greece, where wives were taken solely for the purpose of bearing legitimate children and, in most cases, were treated like dependents and confined to activities such as caring for children, cooking, and keeping house (Ingoldsby 2006). The marriage trends of the elites were often embraced, at least ideologically, by the other social classes, even when they lacked the resources to conform to such ideologies. The focus on legalizing marriage and male domination became common among all classes, although among the less affluent there was less property to transfer to legitimate heirs, and patriarchy was mediated by the contributions of women to the family income.

The Merging of Religion, Law, and Family Life

The growing emphasis on formal marriage contracts and patriarchy was reinforced in Western societies by the influence of Christianity and the law. Christianity was initially seen as a sect of Judaism, but with the conversion of Emperor Constantine in AD 313, it became the established religion and rose to dominate European social life for centuries (Goldthorpe 1987). Christianity may have helped foster monogamy, but it distinguished itself from its forebearer, Judaism, by breaking away from Jewish traditions— which had celebrated married life, marital sexuality, and especially procreation—and providing a more circumspect view of marriage. The exposure of early Christians to the overt sexuality and eroticism that was common in Rome (Coltrane and Adams 2008:49), along with the Apostle Paul's denunciation of marriage and the belief that the return of Jesus was imminent, led church leaders to eschew marriage and teach that celibacy was a higher, more exalted way of life. For many, there was an inherent conflict between pursuing the spirit and satisfying the flesh, and marriage led to the latter. Marriage was allowed, but commonly seen as a union created as the result of original sin. Thus, in most cases, marriage ceremonies had to be held outside the church doors, and a sense of impurity surrounded even marital sex and childbearing (Coltrane and Adams 2008). The marginalization of family life and marriage by early Christianity reinforced traditions that were unique to Western Europe and enhanced the wealth of the Church. Goldthorpe (1987) points out that bilateral kinship, consensual marriages, singleness as a viable option, and the nuclear family structure were common in Western Europe even before the influence of Christianity. But this restricted sense of kinship helped the Church become immensely wealthy, as its teachings discouraged marriage, stated that Christians should put the needs of the Church before family loyalties, and encouraged them to leave their property to the Church rather than to relatives (pp. 12–13).

Around AD 1200, however, there was a reversal of this doctrine. Both Christian leaders and the state began to assume a larger role in defining and governing marriages, and within a century they had declared marriage a sacrament of the Christian Church and an indissolvable union (Yalom 2001; Thornton et al. 2007). Not all Christians accepted the notion of marriage as a sacrament, which essentially placed entering and dissolving marital unions under the control of the Church. Protestantism especially rejected this teaching, and the numerous sects it fostered drew on the Bible to justify a variety of marriage practices, including polygamy. Over time, however, mainstream Christian teachings supporting monogamy, nonmarital chastity, and marital fidelity were seen as strengthening the nuclear family, although they did little to elevate the position of women (Ingoldsby 2006).

As the state and Church initiated efforts to regulate marriage, it became the core of the family; however, the debate over how one entered a legal marriage continued in most Western nations through the early 1900s. People often rejected the idea of religious and state control over marriage or, more practically, simply ignored such rules about licenses and ceremonies because they lived in remote areas that made it difficult for them to avail themselves of bureaucratic procedures. The long tradition of informal marriages—described as "self-marriages" or "living tally"—continued, and it was common for poor people to live as married without benefit of legal ceremony (Cherlin 2009). As Nancy Cott (2000:28) explains, the federal government had few ways to enforce its views on marriage, and state laws varied, often only specifying that marriages could not be bigamous, incestuous, or easily terminated. Thus, although states and religious authorities had been given the authority to perform marriage ceremonies, there was ambiguity over exactly what constituted a legal marriage. The most common bases for declaring marriages valid were mutual consent, cohabitation, and sexual consummation of the relationship, although not all of these criteria had to be met for a legally recognized marriage to exist (Thornton et al. 2007:60).

Institutionalizing Inequalities: Gender and Race

Although defining marriage and enforcing marriage rules were often difficult, there was substantial agreement across cultures on one point: Men were to be the dominant partner in the marriage or the heads of their families, and wives were to be subservient and obedient to their husbands. This gender ideology, of course, evolved over time. Most would contend that it was weakest in early hunting and gathering societies, when there was little reason for men and women to form exclusive sexual relationships or prioritize marriage. Still, the dual burdens of bearing children and engaging in productive labor may have made it more difficult for women to survive alone and led them to attach themselves to men, who took advantage of the weaker position of women by forcing them into subordination (Reuter and Runner 1931). Other theories resonate with this perspective, suggesting that women needed the provision and protection of men and gradually came to trade the exclusive right to their sexuality to men who could provide these things. Coontz (2005) opines, however, that this provider-protector theory of male domination casts women as helpless entities and ignores much evidence of the powerful and productive roles they have played in many societies. Leonard Shlain (2003) also accords women a more active role in creating the gender order. He argues that among early humans, women were first to recognize the link between sex, pregnancy, and childbirth—an important discovery, given that the perils associated with childbearing often cost them their lives. As a result, women managed to break the estrus cycle and, to better their chances of survival, offer sex more selectively to those men who could provide them with more nutritious food (especially meat) and safety.

In all likelihood, a number of biological, economic, and ideological factors—such as the discovery of biological paternity, greater male strength, weapons, surplus wealth, and institutionalized religions—all converged in fostering male domination in marriages and in the broader societies. In settled societies, gender inequality became the norm, although the intensity of it varied based on the ability of societies to differentiate the roles of men and women (Buechler 2008) and the degree to which women were integrated into the work force and the kinship structure of their families of origin (Sanday 1981). Whatever women's actual roles in society, most of the major organized religions support the subordination of women as God-ordained. The Hebrew Scriptures provide a rationale for male dominance in the early chapters: Eve disobeyed God, led her husband to do so, and was punished by God by being placed under the rule of her husband. As Ingoldsby (2006) points out, the Hebrew Scriptures repeatedly reinforce the subordinate status of women; for example, women are included in the list of domestic property that one is forbidden from coveting in the Ten Commandments, labeled as unclean because of menstruation and childbirth, held to a double standard of sexuality, and subjected to divorce for practically any reason given by their husbands (pp. 42–43). The Scriptures, however, have a different set of rules for men: Men can have more than one wife, have a wife who is found not to be a virgin killed, and require strict obedience and even a male child if the marriage is to be sustained (Yalom 2001).

One result has been that since the Middle Ages marriage contracts have deemed men the legal heads of their families and assigned them responsibility for and control over women and families. As Lenore Weitzman (1981) explains, in English law the doctrine of coverture suspended the identity and personhood of a wife, which was legally merged with that of her husband, so in most places she lost control over her own property and wages, the right to enter contracts, and the right to sue or be sued. As the heads of their families, men determined the legal residence for the family and their standard of living; could discipline their wives and command their marital, sexual, and domestic services; and could claim or control their earnings or any property they owned (Reuter and Runner 1931:158).

These patriarchal marital ideals were incompatible with the rise of Enlightenment ideologies during the 1500s. An important element of these ideologies was the rejection of hierarchal and authoritarian relationships, which led to a greater emphasis on liberty and individual freedoms. Although these concepts primarily focused on the political rights and economic freedom of men, they also spawned new thinking about marriage relationships. Men were still held as the natural heads of their families, but many argued that marriages should be monogamous and based on mutual affection and consent. These emerging marital ideologies held that there should be symmetry (although not equality) between married men and their wives in their education and lifestyles and described marriage as the "highest instance of human friendship" and as "loving partnerships" (Cott 2000:16). But overall, Enlightenment thinkers were not inclined to see women and men as equal actors in the social and political arenas or in family life. Most failed to consider how male-headed marriages based on female economic dependence undermined the ideal of women entering marriages based solely on free choice and affection. Moreover, some feminist scholars have argued that the concept of affection-based marriage in many ways devalued kinship and family by making them more optional and elevated the importance of those arenas dominated by men—the market and the state.

Racial and Ethnic Stratification

The concept of race and racial stratification systems also emerged with agricultural societies, where surplus production and expansionist tendencies created an almost insatiable demand for raw materials, labor, and new markets. Although slavery is ancient in origin, the development of agricultural economies led to brutal forms of chattel slavery and colonialism; for example, by the tenth century some Middle Eastern nations had instituted a race-based slavery system, notably the trafficking of black Africans. By the 1400s, Europeans had begun a pattern of international travel and trade that exploited and colonized people of color in India, Asia, Africa, and South America, using them as both cheap labor and markets for Western products (Duiker and Spielvogel 1994). Through colonialist policies, Europeans gained control over the economies in many less-developed nations, placing themselves in positions of power and endowing a handful of locals—usually those who were willing to embrace Western behaviors—with power over other members of the native population (Leeder 2004:95). Howard Winant (2001) argues that the colonist and empire-building practices of Europeans constituted an early global racial formation project that cast native peoples around the world as racial others (pp. 20–25). In the process, whiteness was socially constructed as a racial category, and the most basic divisions became that between being white and non-white, or European and non-European.

Europeans' contact with people of color on other continents, many of whom lacked sophisticated technologies and weapons and had not been exposed to Christianity, fostered ethnocentric attitudes among Europeans; most held themselves and their culture to be naturally superior. Their ethnocentric attitudes provided the rationale for exploiting people of color, who were often seen as less than human but also in need of Christian morality or the civilizing influence of Western culture. These views were reinforced during the 1800s by the social science studies that placed the European ideal of monogamous, nuclear families at the apex of civilization and assumed that all other families were "primitive" or lacking in development (Lamanna 2002). This racial division resulted in negative and even punitive images of most non-Europeans, who were seen as having backward and primitive cultures, and such images justified excluding them from Enlightenment doctrines of natural rights, rationality, and freedom (Winant 2001:72).

Social Inequalities in Colonial America

The Europeans who began to settle in the British colonies of North America in the 1600s came in pursuit of greater economic opportunity and religious freedom and brought with them an implicit faith in the rectitude of their own cultural heritage. The acceptance of social inequalities was part of that heritage, and the class system that emerged in the New World approximated the one that had developed in Europe by the mid-1600s. Historian Howard Zinn ([1980] 2003) explains that during the seventeenth and early eighteenth centuries, more than half the colonists came as servants, many of them forced into exile from Europe in its effort to rid itself of "rogues and vagabonds" (p. 42). As Zinn pointed out, colonial society "was not democratic and certainly not egalitarian; it was dominated by men who had money enough to make others work for them" (p. 46). Populist resentment against the wealthy and elite, which often led to rebellions and riots, was common, and by the 1700s, poor houses were being created to quell the unrest.

Although there was some racial and ethnic diversity in the early colonial population, the majority of the three million white Europeans who came to the colonies from the early 1600s until 1790 were from England (Schaefer 2008), and they set the tone for political and cultural life in the New World. Many who left England—but especially the Puritans who migrated voluntarily—were fleeing from a place where industrialization and modernization was in its early stages and producing unprecedented economic and social changes. One of their goals was pursuing traditional or "Old World" ideas about marriages and families that were in decline in England (Mintz and Kellogg 1988). They wanted to create godly families, defined primarily as patriarchal institutions in which men ruled over their wives, but they also wanted to extend the rights and benefits of marriage to more people (e.g., certain groups of people in England could not marry or inherit property; Zinn and Eitzen 2002:38). Many rejected the rising status of women that had emerged with the industrial economy in England—autonomy that was being gained as a result of high rates of female employment and the growing emphasis on women's property and marital rights—in favor of a society based on religious traditions and a clear gender hierarchy. In their view, married women owed their husbands loyalty and obedience; thus, in early America, a man had "nearly absolute authority over his wife . . . including the right to administer physical correction" (Walsh 1985:4).

But even in the New World, patriarchal ideologies were mitigated by the fact that the productive and reproductive labor of women was much in demand. Women played an important role in establishing the American colonies and endured immense hardships in helping their husbands build and furnish homes and provide for families (Goodsell 1934). The shortage of women—due to the fact that men were more likely to immigrate and women had a high rate of maternal mortality—also increased the value of women. The family-based economy of the agricultural era required the labor of all able-bodied family members, and women played an essential role in the survival of families. Families had a broad array of functions to fulfill and were seen as little commonwealths that were vital to the survival of individuals and the community. The functions of families during that era have been described this way:

[The family] raised the food and made most of the clothing and furniture for
early settlers. It taught children to read, worship their God, and care for each
other in sickness and in old age. It was a workplace, a school, a vocational
training agency, and a place of worship, and it carried the heavy burden of
responsibility for maintaining social order and stability. (Mintz and Kellogg
1988:1)

Thus, marriage was often considered an economic partnership between
men and women, formed to help ensure that the material needs of families
were supplied. This definitely extended the type of work women were able
to perform; in fact, some scholars have held that colonial women could perform any kind of work they wanted to—as long as it was acceptable to their
husbands and understood as helping the family (Ingoldsby 2006).

As the colonial population grew, the rigidity of patriarchal rules in families varied regionally and weakened over time and was especially compromised as the economy transitioned from agriculture to industry. For
example, women in urban areas typically had more freedom than those in
rural areas, and unmarried females had more freedom than married women.
In his study of the journals of Europeans who visited America in the 1800s,
Furstenberg (1966) noted that most commented favorably on the freedom
given to young women, even in matters of courtship and marriage, and the
power and authority that wives often had in the domestic arena. Although
such gender patterns are consistent with Western ideologies of equality and
freedom, they likely attracted attention because gender inequalities were
even more striking in other nations.

Patriarchal rules also influenced the lives of children in colonial America
because fathers were the sole guardians of their children and determined
their education, religious training, and marriages (Goodsell 1934). The prevailing childrearing philosophy, at least among Christians, was that parents
needed to rid children of their innately sinful nature, so severe discipline was
common and in most eastern colonies laws supported the penalty of death
for unruly and obstinate children (Goodsell 1934). This has raised the question of the status of children not just in colonial America, but historically.
Some historians have traced a long history of the abuse and neglect of children in many societies and have argued that parents were not particularly
emotionally attached to their children. Children were often seen as economic
burdens or economic assets, and in the latter case, they were expected to
work and contribute to the support of families.

In colonial America, the view that children were innately sinful and the
high rate of childhood mortality may have created some emotional distance
between parents and children. As Coltrane and Adams (2008) explain,

before the 1900s, more than half of all parents had lost at least one child, and childhood death did not usually result in long periods of grieving (p. 138). Other scholars have contended that parents have always loved and valued their children, although this pattern of parent-child relationship may have been more evident in some regions and time periods than others. By the 1800s, European visitors to America sometimes observed that parents were overly permissive and failed to properly discipline their children (Furstenberg 1966). Social class and regional differences probably resulted in differences in how parents reared their children, and patterns of child-rearing also changed over time as the economy became more industrialized. Parents who did not rely on children to contribute to the support of the family were likely to be more emotionally indulgent and less strict that those who did.

Confronting the Racial "Other"

European explorers had contact with native populations in various parts of the world as early as the 1400s, often in the context of market trade. The decision to settle in areas occupied by native populations, however, posed a new set of challenges as it brought competition for land and natural resources and exposed groups to immense cultural differences. Europeans, for example, defined basic morality largely in terms of their understanding of proper family relations, yet they found themselves in a land inhabited by as many as two million native peoples, or Native Americans, who did not embrace those values. Native Americans had lived in North America for centuries before the arrival of Europeans and were organized in tribes that were extremely diverse: They spoke at least 200 different languages and had a variety of cultural practices (Zinn and Eitzen 2002:37), many of which deviated from European concepts of Christian morality or proper gender relations. Native American women, for example, were often farmers, and European settlers sought to train them in proper European gender roles (Ingoldsby 2006). Native American tribes had a variety of family systems; they often married during early adolescence, sometimes without ceremony, and many practiced polygamy. In quite a few tribes, descent was traced through mothers, and women were producers who owned property and held high-status positions. Europeans often described these marriage practices as "unintelligibly foreign," according to historian Cott (2000), and believed that Native American men, who were hunters but did not exert much authority over their families or cultivate or own land, were simply unmanly and lazy (p. 25).

The diversity of family practices Europeans encountered among indigenous tribes in North America reinforced the views of colonists that there was widespread savagery among native populations and that they had a mandate to spread order, civilization, and Christianity through missionary work, legislation, and coercion (Thornton 2005). Despite their view of Native Americans as deficient, whites reasoned that it was possible to civilize the tribes by spreading Christianity and the virtues of European culture. Efforts were made to convince Native Americans to accept monogamous marriage, a conventional sexual division of labor, and the concepts of private property and inheritance (Cott 2000:26). Many Native Americans complied with these efforts, while others resisted, engaged in warfare, and eventually were decimated or moved to reservations (Thornton 2005).

African American Families

Racial diversity in the colonies was also enhanced by the growing number of Africans being brought to the continent. During the early 1600s, Africans were already beginning to arrive in the New World, some as indentured servants. Indentured servitude for Africans, however, was gradually transformed into perpetual servitude, or a system of slavery based on race and heredity. Winant (2001) argues that the investment in slaves was the first and largest capital investment of the era, and slavery was the "motor" of early capitalist development (p. 47). By 1790, when the first census was taken, there were 750,000 Africans living in the country—20 percent of the entire population—and 90 percent of them were slaves (Mintz and Kellogg, 1988).

Enslaved blacks brought with them a variety of family practices from pre-colonial West African societies, some of which paralleled those found in the New World (e.g., patriarchal ideology, economically productive roles for women, high rates of fertility) and others which were different (e.g., polygamy, early sexuality and marriage, extended kin relations). Slavery prioritized the labor roles of Africans over their family roles and, in the process, reinforced African family practices that did not resonate with Christian or mainstream American values. Indeed, many abolitionists argued that the worst abuse of slavery was its "outrage upon the families" of black people and accused Southern slaveholders of breeding slaves like oxen and of maintaining "black harems" of sexually exploited black women (Mintz and Kellogg 1988: 67, 77).

Slavery inherently undermined the ability of Africans to form stable families because slaves were considered property and slave owners could treat them and sell them as they saw fit. Researchers have found that the family life of slaves varied over the duration of slavery and from region to region, with the size the plantation and the economic solvency of slaveholders shaping the stability of family life: Overall, slaveholders owning smaller, more economically marginal plantations offered a limited supply of potential partners for marriage. As Mintz and Kellogg (1988) explain, the majority of slave owners in the South had fewer than 20 slaves, most of them related to each other. In addition, slaveholders with only a few slaves were more likely to have to sell slaves and separate families and were more likely to engage in sexual liaisons with enslaved blacks (Franklin 1997). Even when enslaved *families* achieved stability, *marriages* tended to be more difficult to enter into and sustain. During the early decades of slavery, a skewed sex ratio—considerably more men than women—made it impossible for all men to find marital partners. But even on larger plantations, at least one-third of husbands had wives who lived elsewhere and were often restricted to weekend visits (Mintz and Kellogg 1988).

Enslaved Africans in Northern areas often did not fare much better when it came to creating stable marriages and families. Northern slaveholders usually owned fewer slaves; in 1790, half of them owned only one slave (Dabel 2002). This scarcity of blacks was compounded by the fact that many Northern slaveholders preferred to own enslaved women who were single and childless, or at least whose children were living elsewhere. This lowered rates of marriage among black women: Jane Dabel found, for example, that among black women living in New York between 1850 and 1870, two-thirds were unmarried. Equally important in undermining marriage was the fact that slave marriages had no legal sanction, and couples could be separated or sold at the discretion of slaveholders.

Even when marriages existed, the property status of blacks and the arduous labor demanded of men and women made it impossible for them to create families that adhered to mainstream values. Although enslaved Africans accepted the ideology of patriarchal families, it was difficult for men to achieve authority in their families when they lived on other plantations, had little control over how their wives and children were provided for, and could not protect them from the abuses of slavery. Like men, enslaved women were defined first and foremost as laborers, and they typically found extended kin networks a more reliable source of help with children than marriage. Most enslaved black women worked in the fields and counted on others to watch their children. Those who were domestic workers garnered a certain status and social-cultural capital from their close association with white families, and such workers tended to be women. This further undermined male domination among enslaved Africans and elevated the status of black women who performed domestic work; they often had access to better food, which they could share with other family members, and were privy to vital information about events and issues on the plantation (Jones 1985; Hine and Thompson 1998).

The families of free black people, most of whom had once been slaves, still bore the mark of slavery, including precarious race relations and a fragile economic standing. Prior to the Civil War, there were about 250,000 free blacks living in the country, and most of them had either been freed or escaped from slavery (Mintz and Kellogg 1988). Free blacks occupied an ambiguous space between slavery and freedom, with enforced segregation affecting most areas of life and restricting their rights and movements. A significant number of free blacks lived in single-mother families, as women were more likely than men to be free. Studying the family life of free blacks who lived in Norfolk, Virginia, prior to abolition, Bogger (1997) reported that families were almost equally likely to be headed by men as women, although this may have been because free men commonly left the area in search of work. Those who stayed held a variety of occupations and, with a bounty of women to choose from, often had wives who were much younger than they were. These families performed the same functions as other colonial families, with the added responsibility of helping friends and family members gain their freedom.

Industrialization and the Modern Family

Industrialization began in England in the eighteenth century, displacing thousands of agricultural workers, creating family-based cottage systems of industry that drew on the labor of the entire family, and ultimately downgrading the lives of millions of Europeans. Felix Greene (1971), for example, writes that starting in the late 1700s, thousands of Enclosure Acts were passed that dispossessed people of their land and livelihood and created human suffering beyond imagination. According to Greene,

> The emergence of a huge, property-less and impoverished working class was precisely what the new industrialists wished for. They could, and did, dictate their own conditions. . . . For wages that would barely keep them alive, workers were herded into huge slums that had no sewerage, no adequate water supply, no beauty, no cultural amenities, no playgrounds. The company-built hovels in which they had to live were of such meanness that today it would be illegal to use them to house animals. (P. 92)

By the mid-nineteenth century, the industrial economy was struggling to meet the demands of the new markets being opened around the world, and factories sprang up in cities and towns. Children and women were often as capable as men of operating the machinery in factories, and they entered the factory labor system in large numbers. This potential for economic independence altered families by making children less reliant on families for their survival and women freer from male domination. By the mid-1800s, the notion that women "had minds and characters worthy of broad and thorough training" was gaining strength, and longstanding laws making married men the sole legal guardians of their children and giving them control over the property of their wives were being challenged and changed (Goodsell 1934).

The Spread of Industrialization to the New World

This economic transition and the liberal ideologies that were emerging helped fuel the migration of more Europeans to the New World. Although some were simply uprooted by the new economic order, others sought to create a society in which traditional marital and family ideologies would prevail. But by the mid-1800s, the U.S. economy was also undergoing industrialization, and by 1900, it had emerged as the world's leading industrial nation (Gilbert 2003). This economic transition took more than a century and resulted in massive social, geographical, and family changes. Industrialization shifted populations from rural to urban areas in search of work; for example, in 1830 most Americans still lived in rural areas and were employed in farming, but by 1930, most lived in towns and cities and were engaged in non-farming occupations (p. 51). Urbanization, immigration, and adjustment to the industrial labor market took a toll on the stability of families. Industrial production undermined the family-based economy, food production technologies reduced the need for farmers, and essentials once produced by families were now produced in massive quantities in factories. New professional institutions emerged (e.g., public schools, hospitals) and assumed responsibility for many of the functions once fulfilled by families, ultimately making people less dependent on the family and leading some social scientists to predict its demise.

The industrial economy is linked to a social class system of stratification, in which mobility is possible and ostensibly based on effort and hard work. The industrial economy resulted in substantial wealth, but neither wealth nor the opportunity to acquire it was distributed equally in the population. As had been the case in Europe, the first decades of industrialization produced downward mobility for most men; in 1870, and for the first time in U.S. history, more men were working for other people than for themselves, often with little control over their workday or wages (Buechler 2008:146).

The industrial laborers who composed the working class toiled long hours for low wages in working conditions that were deplorable and dangerous; for example, in 1897 the average work week was 60 hours, and a survey conducted in 1907 found that at the very least, a half million workers had been killed, crippled, or seriously injured on the job (Gilbert 2003:55). Although working conditions improved over time, by the 1920s, the living conditions for the majority of workers were still poor (Hurst 2004:317). Goodsell (1934:493) wrote that in 1927, 41 million of the 45 million employed Americans were exempt from filing income reports with the federal government because their earnings were too low to be taxed. Workers were frequently in conflict with employers over working conditions and unfair labor practices, and by the turn of the twentieth century, worker strikes had become common.

Racial and Ethnic Inequality in Industrial America

The challenge of adapting to the industrial economy was further complicated by a rapid increase in the racial and ethnic diversity of the population. The majority of the nearly three million people who immigrated to the United States between 1800 and 1850 were from the eastern and southern regions of Europe (Mintz and Kellogg 1988) and, based on the dominant English notion of race, they were not considered "white" and thus were seen as a social and economic threat. Even more threatening than the influx of white ethnics was the growing population of people of color. Much of that racial diversity was a result of territorial expansion: In 1845, John O'Sullivan declared that it was the manifest destiny of white Europeans to "overspread the continent allotted by Providence for the free development of our yearly multiplying millions," and a few years later, the United States purchased New Mexico, California, and Texas from Mexico for the price of $15 million (Zinn [1980] 2003:151–153). In addition, there were 200,000 Chinese who had migrated to the United States between 1850 and 1880, many in search of gold or the new jobs that were opening in the western region of the country (Schaefer 2008). Their entry into the labor market sparked intense competition for jobs and eventually led to the passage by Congress in 1882 of the Chinese Exclusion Act, which prohibited immigration from China. Chinese, along with other Asians who came to the United States, found themselves in a racially stratified labor market, where skin color predicted position more than did education or skills. By the 1920s, additional restrictive immigration policies were passed that favored immigrants from northern Europe (Schaefer 2008).

The release of four million African Americans from slavery in the 1860s added to the racial diversity of the new labor force, although most remained in the rural South and worked in the rapidly declining agricultural economy. Few economic opportunities were available for the newly freed slaves, and many who left the homes of their former owners found themselves adrift, homeless, and facing starvation. The majority of former slaves, however, moved into a sharecropping system, with living and working conditions— and wages—that closely resembled slavery. The threat posed by the loss of black labor led some states to create and enforce labor contracts between black workers and white land owners, justifying them on the premise that employment was essential to the transition from slavery to citizenship (Franklin 2000). In many cases, African Americans who had skilled positions lost their jobs after emancipation, as racial fears, threats and rumors of racial insurrections, and negative racial images intensified. African Americans in some Southern states gained political rights during the era of Reconstruction, but those measures were being rapidly repealed by the latter nineteenth century: In 1896, scarcely 30 years after the abolition of slavery, the *Plessy v. Ferguson* decision made segregation the law of the land. By the turn of the twentieth century, Southern racial violence, the waning agricultural economy, and the lure of factory jobs in cities sparked a massive shift in the black population from the rural South to the urban North.

Racial stratification characterized the labor market until after the civil rights era of the 1960s, with most African Americans being firmly at the bottom of the occupational hierarchy. Still, the first iteration of the black middle class had emerged after slavery and was mostly composed of light-skinned African Americans who were heirs and/or direct beneficiaries of white slave owners. Other racial/ethnic groups fared little better: Asian Americans, many of whom were highly skilled and educated, were working as grocers and gardeners (Sakamoto et al. 2009).

Gender in Industrial America

The reorganization of work in the industrial economy disrupted the gender order of many families by pulling women into the paid labor force and spawning new visions of gender equality. As had been the case in England, American women, especially those who were young and single, entered the labor market in substantial numbers. In the textile mills of Lowell, Massachusetts, for example, women made up nearly 75 percent of all employees and they worked more than 70 hours a week, often in deplorable working conditions (Hurst, 2004:61). Although women were legally paid less than men, and therefore still benefited economically by marrying, the growing ability of single women to earn a living made many, especially those who were educated, reconsider the value of marriage. Many women came to rely on themselves and enjoy the freedom of independence, and the rate of marriage decreased with industrialization. New ideologies of marriage based on free choice, romantic love, and companionship spread and led to a surge in the divorce rate, which more than tripled between the late 1860s and 1910 (Cherlin, 1992). Goodsell (1934), for example, noted that in 1885 alone more marriages were dissolved in the United States than in all the rest of the Christian world combined. Married couples increasingly expected their marriages to be based on companionship, affection, and partnership, and were less likely to tolerate unfulfilling marriages.

Notably, the first wave of feminism emerged during the mid-1800s, with many women demanding the right to vote, participate in public life, own property, use birth control, attend college, and control their own bodies (Calhoun 1997). For the most part, however, early feminism did not challenge dominant ideologies about marriage, family, or the breadwinner-homemaker division of labor (Gordon 1976). Women, especially those who were married to economically affluent men, found it prestigious to be exempt from productive labor, provided for by their husbands, and free to devote their time to the care of their children and homes. Affluent women often saw gender equality in the public arena as a threat to the family (Camhi 2007), and many who supported education and reproductive rights for women did so because they believed that these rights would enable women to be better wives and mothers. The major barrier to the acceptance and creation of breadwinner-homemaker families was simply the inability of many husbands to adequately support their wives. Thus, racial/ethnic minority, working-class, and poor families endured the most strains in trying to conform to the male wage-earner family model, but cycles of economic depression often challenged the viability of this family model for middle-class couples.

The Sociological Study of Families

Early sociologists were primarily interested in understanding processes of modernity, the massive reorganization of society caused by industrialization and resulting in migration, urbanization, greater racial and ethnic diversity, and processes of assimilation. They saw social institutions, including families, as being transformed by these new economic and social forces and, given escalating rates of family instability, divorce, and non-marriage in the late nineteenth century, many feared the demise of families. Moreover, families seemed to be losing important functions as societies modernized and marriage became optional rather than essential for survival. By the mid-1940s, with the American economy back on track and experiencing massive growth, concern over the demise of families was slowly being replaced by a celebration of the superiority of modern families as inherently middle class and based on a breadwinner-homemaker division of labor.

Talcott Parsons, perhaps the best-known family sociologist of the era, surmised that while the economic instability of the early twentieth century had adversely affected families, it had ultimately given rise to stronger, more specialized families (Parsons and Bales 1955). Whereas kinship structures dominate in primitive societies because they are necessary for survival, Parsons theorized that advanced societies underwent a process of structural differentiation that resulted in the creation of more non-kinship structures (e.g., churches, states, schools), each of which performed specialized functions (Parsons and Bales 1955:9). In the process, families had released most of their macro- or societal-level functions and were now free to take on more specialized micro-level functions, namely, the personality development of children and the social and emotional needs of spouses. Influenced by Freudian psychology and emerging research on the adverse consequences of maternal deprivation, Parsons was persuaded that the human personality was not inborn, but rather was constructed through elaborate family socialization processes, and that families also functioned to maintain and stabilize adult personalities. Families that functioned well were also specialized internally, with men taking on an occupational role and women a homemaker role. Although women may be in the labor market, especially those who are single, divorced, widowed, or childless, Parsons argued that there could be "no question of symmetry between the sexes in this respect, and . . . there is no serious tendency in this direction" (Parsons and Bales 1955:14).

The Modern Isolated Nuclear Family

The modern family was seen primarily as a nuclear, marriage-based entity in which men provided economically for their families and women performed housework and took care of children. This gender division of family responsibility, described as the *doctrine of separate spheres,* held that men belonged in the public arena (or world of work) and women in the private arena, or the home. Socially defined notions of masculinity and femininity reflected these gendered family roles; for example, men were characterized as being naturally aggressive and rational—traits valuable in the competitive area of work—and women as being essentially submissive, domestic, and nurturing. Based on what has been described as the *cult of true womanhood,* women were endowed with a higher sense of purity and morality than men. The breadwinner-homemaker family model was more available to economically affluent European American families, but by the early 1950s, several factors—the rise of labor unions and the demand that men be paid family wage—heightened access to this family model. Parsons and Bales (1955) described modern families as "isolated" because they were nuclear in structure (composed of parents and children); performed a limited, specific set of functions; and were less reliant on or connected to the broader kinship structures. Parsons opined that kinship dominated social structures in "primitive" societies, whereas non-kinship structures were dominant in "advanced" societies.

The notion of successful child socialization as a key function of the family, along with the reduced need for the economic labor of children as industrialization advanced, reshaped dominant attitudes and ideologies about children. Children in modern, middle-class families were increasingly seen as emotional rather than economic assets and as belonging more to mothers than to fathers. Endowed with this new sentimental value, they were the heart of the family, and being a good parent (or mother) required learning about child development and devoting considerable energy to socializing children. Whether or not childhood existed as a distinct stage of life in earlier societies, it was now clearly a prolonged period of life that included adolescence, a stage at which children began to negotiate their adult identities. Theories of child development proliferated during the early twentieth century, such as those proposed by psychologist Sigmund Freud and sociologist George Herbert Mead. Most saw children as moving through specific stages of development, propelled by both biological and social forces, and more emphasis was placed on their physical, social, and psychological needs. Legislators passed laws aimed at protecting and investing in children, such as mandatory education and policies ensuring their welfare, and many parents no longer saw rearing children as something that just came naturally.

More affluent families responded to this redefinition of children as precious and as requiring extensive parental investment by having fewer of them but investing more resources and time in raising each child. The fertility rate declined from six children per family in 1840 to three per family in 1900 (Kline 2001). Lower infant mortality rates also helped pave the way to reduced rates of childbearing, as did more effective birth control and the voluntary motherhood movement, although the underlying ideologies supporting controlled fertility differed. Birth control advocates argued for the right of women to control their fertility by using contraceptive technologies, thus enhancing the quality of life for women and the physical and mental endowments of children (Gordon 1976). Those embracing the voluntary motherhood movement rejected birth control but argued that women should have the right to control their fertility by refusing sexual intercourse with their husbands, a move which promised to enable women to gain more control over their bodies, sexuality, and fertility. Overall, the notion of middle-class, child-centered, nuclear families headed by wage-earning husbands became the ideal, although making that family model the norm for most Americans took decades and then was short-lived.

Middle-Class America: Realities, Myths, and Transitions

The road to middle-class America and the breadwinner-homemaker family ideal was a bumpy one, often interrupted by the vagaries of the capitalist market and the onset of wars and exclusive of large segments of the population. The most notable economic challenge was the Great Depression of the 1930s, which resulted in widespread job loss and poverty, delayed marriages, and the entry of many women into the labor market. The causes of the Great Depression are still debated—the over-extension of credit, stock market and real estate speculation—but the consequences were clear: Between 1929 and 1933, businesses failed, fortunes were lost, real wages declined by at least one-third, unemployment increased, and 45–63 percent of the population lived in poverty (Ryscavage 2009:90–92). The economic decline curtailed marriage and fertility rates and drew more women into the labor market, fostering new images of women as more independent and self-sufficient. Elaine Tyler May (1999:35) argues that it resulted in a spate of media images depicting women as spunky, sensual, strong, autonomous, competent, and career oriented. The onset of World War II further increased labor market participation by women; many were drawn into the labor market to replace men who were off at war, and they were applauded as patriotic by the new "Rosie the Riveter" image of womanhood.

The industrial production that occurred during World War II revitalized the U.S. economy due to the demand for workers and products, making it the strongest economy in the world. After the War ended, government intervention, growing rates of education, and the unionization of labor resulted in a blurring of the class line between the working and middle classes and a period of economic growth that was unprecedented in history (Marger 2008). The government offered an expanded array of social welfare benefits, such as unemployment compensation, and the Serviceman's Readjustment Act of 1944 (or GI Bill of Rights) offered extensive benefits for veterans, including housing, insurance, and educational benefits. High school completion rates nearly doubled between 1930 and 1950, the number of college degrees attained increased fourfold, and there was a notable expansion of both white-collar and skilled blue-collar jobs (Ryscavage 2009). In 1956, the Interstate Highway Act authorized $100 billion to cover most of the cost of a 41,000-mile national highway system, thus facilitating the move to the suburbs. New homes, automobiles, and television sets became the norm for many Americans, but as May (1999) explains,

> Consumerism in the post-war years went far beyond the mere purchases of goods and services. It included important cultural values, demonstrated success and social mobility, and defined lifestyles. It also provided the most visible symbol of the American way of life: the affluent suburban home. (P. 162)

This post-war affluence made the 1950s the heyday of the modern nuclear family, a family ideal that spread well beyond national borders in its influence. Because the United States had become the world's hegemonic society, sociologists primarily studied American families and saw them as a model for other societies (Wallerstein 2004). The modern nuclear family came to epitomize economically successful family life and the fruits of capitalism, and even those left out of the economic bounty were seen as holding values that would soon enable them to enjoy a middle-class lifestyle. For example, a family textbook written by Andrew G. Truxal and Francis E. Merrill and published in 1947 overtly and repeatedly compares the American family favorably with other families. Although they acknowledged economic disparities, they asserted that American families ("excluding Negroes") were middle-class families because they held the same values, defined themselves as middle class, and were rapidly transitioning into that class (pp. 23–25). The authors make clear the connection between capitalism and the creation of successful families by noting that Americans are as capitalistic in their family affairs as in business, leading to an "all-pervasive individualism and emancipation from traditional dictates and familial domination" (p. 79). Finally, while evading the issue of gender equality in marriage, they contended that modernity had elevated the social status of women, making it necessary for men to offer women quite a bit to marry them and "willingly submit to economic subordination" (p. 174).

The United States dominated the world economy in the three decades following World War II, controlling two-thirds of its industrial capacity and 75 percent of its invested capital (Perrucci and Wysong 2007). Although the growing prosperity of Americans in the post-war era has been widely documented, it was not shared by all segments of the population. By the early 1960s, among those who were employed, nearly 80 percent of African American men and 49 percent of white men held blue-collar or working-class jobs (Komarovsky 1962), quite in contrast to popular images of white-collar, suburban families. The poverty rate among African Americans in the late 1950s was more than 50 percent and taking a devastating toll on families. After centuries of slavery and family separation, many black families had been further destabilized by northward migration, joblessness, and a growing trend toward non-marital childbearing and single motherhood. But poverty was not confined to African Americans: In *The Other America,* Michael Harrington (1962) unveiled the existence of more than 30 million people who lived in poverty in the United States—the wealthiest nation on earth. Harrington characterized this poverty as intergenerational in nature and as producing a distinct culture of poverty. This work played a central role in creating the antipoverty programs during the mid-1960s, which tried to alleviate poverty through the creation of jobs and job training. The era marked a high point of idealism among Americans, as millions embraced the notion that poverty would be eliminated. But within a decade, there was a political backlash against government intervention on behalf of the poor and other marginalized groups, intensified by the growing threat to the middle class caused by the rise of the global economy, declining corporate profits, and the transition from an industrial to an information and services economy.

The Post-Industrial Economy and Growing Class Inequality

The rise of the post-industrial, or information and services, economy initially led to a decline in corporate profits in dominant countries like the United States and Britain. This economic decline was met with the emergence of conservative political and economic revolutions in both nations that focused on shrinking the state, cutting social welfare programs, and reviving the capitalist economy (Irwin 2008). These ideals are part of a neoliberal ideology that essentially supports freeing capitalism and individual entrepreneurs from governmental control and restrictions and supporting free markets, free trade, and individual property rights (Harvey 2005). The results have been economic policies and tax structures that redistribute wealth to the wealthy, enable corporations to curtail or cancel fringe benefits for employees, undermine unions, and subsidize companies that transfer jobs abroad

(Bartlett and Steele 1992). Such policies were seen as restoring dynamism to capitalism; for example, the U.S. share of profits in the financial sector rose from 14 percent in 1981 to nearly 40 percent at the turn of the twenty-first century (Irwin 2008).

Few Americans, however, have shared in the economic fortunes of corporations. Instead, the economic transition has displaced millions of workers, starting with those in blue-collar and less skilled positions. As Perrucci and Wysong (2007) explain, more than 11 million American workers lost their jobs between 1978 and 1986 due to plant shutdowns, relocations, and lay-offs, and massive layoffs continued through the early years of the twenty-first century. This restructuring began with the loss of blue-collar jobs in the manufacturing sector and expanded to include the downsizing of the white-collar and managerial sector of the labor market, with corporate mergers, buyouts, and the rise of multinational corporations intent on maximizing profits by investing abroad. At the same time, the pay and fortunes of CEOs and corporate executives skyrocketed during the 1980s and 1990s, as did corporate profits. Perrucci and Wysong present the radical argument that the American middle class no longer exists, as the concept of "middle class" suggests a stable, secure job with adequate resources and benefits (p. 38).

Although opinions may vary on whether there is a stable or viable middle class, there is little dispute over the fact that the middle class has declined, social inequality and class polarization have intensified, and more people have joined the ranks of the working poor. The post-industrial economy has resulted in more social inequality in developed nations; for example, in the United Kingdom, the richest 20 percent of the population earned four times as much as the poorest 20 percent in 1977 but seven times as much by 1991 (Atkinson 2005:54). All developed nations have seen growing class polarization, with the highest levels of social inequality among developed nations found in the United States. Between 1979 and 1997, after-tax income declined for the lowest 20 percent of households, increased just 5 percent in the middle, and grew more than 250 percent for the top 1 percent of earners (Atkinson 2005). There is also evidence that class awareness is increasing among Americans; for example, a majority are concerned about the possibility of losing their jobs and believe that the American Dream has become more difficult to achieve (Perrucci and Wysong 2007). By the 1970s, this had led to renewed debates over class and class theory, which is the topic of Chapter 2.

2

Theorizing
Social Inequalities

S ocial inequality is ubiquitous, practically as old as humankind, and cross-culturally has been more the rule than the exception. As noted in the previous chapter, the emergence of settled agricultural societies, the concept of privately owned land, and surplus wealth coincided with the rise of institutionalized patterns of social inequality based on social class, gender, and race. Social inequalities, whether based on wealth, social class, gender, race, ethnicity, or individual talent, arise with the recognition of biological, social, and cultural differences among people. More important than the mere recognition of the differences that exist among people, however, are the social evaluations of those differences. Such evaluations become the basis for assigning value, status, and privilege to human beings and groups and, once they are widely accepted, the basis for constructing ideologies that rationalize and perpetuate social inequalities. Over time, all societies developed institutionalized patterns of social inequality that resulted in differential access to material resources, status, and power. Even hunting and gathering societies, despite lacking surplus wealth and often even the notion of private property, may have assigned people different statuses based on characteristics such as age, sex, or ability. As societies become more diverse, stable, populous, and wealthy, the prospects for social inequality increase due to greater awareness of the social, cultural, and biological differences between people.

Historically, people often accepted social inequality as ordained by God or as a result of innate differences between people, or some combination of the two. For example, monarchs are seen as having royal blood, and it was once believed that their authority and power were divinely bestowed. Other social thinkers, like Plato, argued that people were placed in the social division of labor according to their natural aptitude and abilities and that in a "good society"—a society that was efficient and stable—people recognized and accepted the inevitability of social inequalities (Rossides 1997). By the Enlightenment era of the 1700s, religious and biological explanations of social inequality were challenged by social thinkers who shifted the focus to a more social-environmental perspective on social inequality. The foundation for this new approach rested in the growing belief that the rights of individuals and families should take precedence over state rights and the rule of monarchs because people were endowed with natural rights and capacities and were, by the very fact of being human, equal by nature. Notable among Enlightenment thinkers was Jean Jacques Rousseau, who in the mid-1700s offered an environmental explanation of social inequality. Based on their original constitution, Rousseau argued, people were essentially alike, but their nature was distorted and corrupted by the social injustices and inequalities that they experienced (Rossides 1997).

Nineteenth-century sociologists held varying beliefs about whether inequality was based on biological or social-environmental factors, many believing that both factors were important. August Comte, the nominal founder of sociology, believed that men naturally fell into one of three categories—brain men, sensory men, and motor men—and that each category had special functions to perform in society. Women were absent from Comte's explicit theorizing about social inequality, but his thinking reflected the sexism of his day: He held that women lived in a "state of perpetual infancy" and were unfit for the "continuousness and intensity of mental labor" (Adams and Steinmetz 1993). Early sociologists were often influenced by Charles Darwin's *On the Origin of Species* and embraced the notion that societies were evolving in the same manner as biological organisms; that is, societies were also moving from simple to complex, with some forms of life becoming extinct because they were not able to compete in new environments. Herbert Spencer, for example, argued that the only way to identify the innate abilities of people was to watch how they adjusted to and fared in competitive situations. Spencer believed the rising market economy and diminishing role of the state fostered such competitive conditions, and people would succeed or fail based on their own capabilities and efforts (Hurst 2004). He coined the phrase "survival of the fittest," noting that it was natural that, as societies evolved, the weaker components would fall away and stronger ones be preserved.

By the early twentieth century, the social-environmental perspective had become dominant in sociology, although lapsing into biological thinking about social inequality (especially when it came to women and racial minorities) was not uncommon. This chapter is devoted to examining how social inequalities, especially as they are related to families, have been theorized by sociologists and other social scientists. *Social theories* are sets of concepts and premises that are used to explain and predict social phenomena. Most of the early or classical theories, written primarily by white men living in Western societies, have a European Caucasian bias (Adams and Steinmetz 1993:71). Rarely did such theories deal seriously with race/ethnicity or gender because such inequalities were likely to be seen as natural and inevitable. It is also important to remember that social theories reflect the dominant concerns of social thinkers during specific historical eras and thus are rarely, if ever, completely free of ideology or "a value judgment that something is good, right, valuable, or is bad, wrong, negative" (p. 75).

Social scientists have a number of theories that can be used to explain families and social inequalities, and the boundaries between those theories are sometimes fairly nebulous. I focus on the three major sociological theories—structural functionalism, conflict theory, and symbolic interactionism—because of their dominance in the field and applicability to issues of social inequality and families. Structural functionalism and conflict theory are usually seen as the two great rival theories in sociology (R. Collins 1975), one focusing on inequality as legitimate and functional in producing order and stability in society and the other emphasizing the unfairness of inequality and its role in generating conflict and change. The social revolutions of the 1960s and 1970s led to the demise of structural functionalism, yet it continued to inform family studies longer than other areas of sociology (R. Collins 1975; Osmond and Thorne 1993). The longevity of structural functionalism in the field of family sociology is partially due to the fact that it shared with another major theory, symbolic interactionism, a common research focus: the study of sex roles and marital adjustment. Symbolic interactionism brought to family studies an emphasis on marital issues such as communication and marital interaction; indeed, Christopher Lasch (1977) argues that by the 1940s, research on most other family issues had practically disappeared from the literature, eclipsed by efforts to define, predict, and measure marital happiness. But by the 1970s, conflict theory had emerged as a perspective in family studies and, along with symbolic interactionism, was being used as a more critical lens that focused on racial and gender inequalities among and within families.

Structural Functionalism

Structural functionalism originated among early twentieth-century anthro-pologists who studied the social customs of non-European populations and explained those customs in terms of their functional role in their respective societies (Ingoldsby, Smith, and Miller 2004). This perspective was also influenced by the evolutionary paradigm that had emerged in the biological sciences, especially the notion that biological organisms had evolved from simple to complex in structure, with each part having a specific function that contributed to the maintenance of the whole. Sociologists were inspired by the logic of the structural functional paradigm and embraced it to advance their understanding of the societal transformations that were resulting from industrialization. Earlier concerns about the adverse consequences of the new industrial economy eventually gave way to the vision of Western societ-ies undergoing an evolutionary process toward greater complexity, with social institutions (such as families) becoming increasingly differentiated and specialized in their function. This explicit emphasis on evolution was eventu-ally embodied in a developmental perspective that saw societies as evolving from traditional to modern, with the latter representing the highest level of civilization. Developmental theory was fostered by individualism, the free market economy, and Christianity, all of which were seen as advancing unique marital trends in Western societies, such as nuclear households, delayed marriage, low fertility rates, and a higher status for women (Goldthorpe 1987; Thornton et al. 2007).

Sociologist Emile Durkheim contributed a broad range of scholarly work to the field of sociology, including studies of the family, and played a central role in developing the structural functional paradigm in sociology. Durkheim believed that the family was the "germ from which society [was] born" and was thus "a complete social organism, which was once self-sufficient and the whole society" (Adams and Steinmetz 1993:88). Unlike other social theo-rists, Durkheim was not concerned that families were becoming obsolete or unimportant in modern, industrial societies; however, as a moralist he was convinced that the traditional basis for solidarity and cohesion among peo-ple was eroded by these forces (Lamanna 2002). In preindustrial societies, solidarity had rested heavily on commonalities—people had similar values and lifestyles—but modernity had produced much more diversity. Durkheim concluded that the division of labor in modern societies, as social institutions came to specialize in different functions, would create social solidarity through interdependence. In fact, he held that the basic gender-based divi-sion of labor in families had now moved into the broader society, specifically in the division of labor in the marketplace, where it served the same purpose as it did in families—fostering interdependence and social solidarity (Adams and Steinmetz 1993:88).

Structural Functionalism and Social Inequality

For the most part, structural functionalists did not see social inequalities, whether based on race, gender, or social class, as much of a problem. Emerging in an era when the new industrial economy was burgeoning and improving the quality of life for most people—and, in some cases, creating massive fortunes—structural functionalists assumed economic opportunity and mobility would be the norm. With immigrants flooding the country in search of work and the American ideology that anyone could succeed through hard work and effort, it was easy to assume that economic hardship could be easily overcome. This became even more the case with the economic prosperity that followed World War II.

During the mid-twentieth century, structural functionalists proffered a theory of social class inequality that resonated strongly with classical economic theory: They saw it largely as a result of supply and demand and the human capital (e.g., education, skills, intelligence) individuals brought to the labor market. Some positions required more sacrifice, skills, and investment than others and deserved to be better compensated. This idea was articulated in a popular article written by Kingsley Davis and Wilbert Moore in the mid-1940s—an era when few Americans were concerned about the supply of jobs available for those willing to work hard. Davis and Moore (1944) argued that there was a universal necessity for social stratification systems. According to these theorists, social inequality was an "unconsciously devised system" that differentially rewarded workers based on two factors: the importance of their job and, in accordance with the principles of supply and demand, the availability of workers who were willing to fill the position.

Social class inequality could become problematic, however, if economic position was based on factors such as inheritance and favoritism rather than merit. Durkheim, for example, believed that the maintenance of social solidarity depended on people being placed in positions that were suited to their abilities and talents (Lehmann 1995). Still, there was little concern among structural functionalists about the relegation of people of color to low-status jobs or the exclusion of women from the labor market. As Jennifer Lehmann has explained, theorists like Durkheim held fairly essentialist views of people of color and women and believed their secondary statuses were consistent with their nature and abilities. Sex role theory dominated, and the focus on the necessity of women as full-time homemakers muted criticism of gender inequality.

Structural Functionalism and the Family

Structural functionalism theorized families through the lens of macro-level economic, evolutionary, and developmental forces that were fostering modernity in all institutions. Families were among those social institutions being modernized: The family had lost many of its traditional functions, but it also was taking on new functions. Structural functionalists held that the structure of families should be compatible with their new functions if they were to operate optimally in the urban, industrial society. Talcott Parsons saw the ideal family structure as an isolated nuclear family, a streamlined family devoid of significant extended family ties, and one based on a bread-winner-homemaker division of labor. In the modern capitalist labor market, this gender division of labor freed men to concentrate on occupational success in an increasingly competitive world and women on the nurturing and development of children. This proposed family structure was the basis for sex role theory, which held that men should assume "instrumental" or wage-earning functions in families and women should assume "expressive" functions, or operate in the private arena of family and care for the social-emotional needs of family members (Parsons and Bales 1955). Such a family model was functional in meeting both the economic and emotional needs of family members, and it also reflected the principles of solidarity, interdependence, and democracy. Married men and women were bound together not only by relationships that were based on affection and free choice, but also because they fulfilled different but complimentary functions. Some functionist theorists held that even romantic love itself was a functional necessity, a kind of social glue that evolved to preserve families and the social stratification system.

Although support for structural functionalism had waned considerably by the 1970s, its significance in family studies can hardly be overstated. One reason for its lasting appeal is that structural functionalism (unlike other social theories) embodied a popular set of value judgments and ideologies: specifically, the belief in solidarity, morality, order, and the intrinsic gratification that comes from conforming to social roles and expectations (Kingsbury and Scanzoni 1993). But its narrow and essentialist view of the roles of women, who were relegated to the domestic arena, proved problematic. While not ignoring women, Laslett and Thorne (1997) argued that structural functionalism held that it was simply dysfunctional for marriage, society, and families for women to participate in the public arena (p. 10). Similarly, structural functionalism implicitly stigmatized working-class and racial/ethnic minority families, many of whom lacked the economic resources needed to create the widely heralded male wage-earner family.

From the perspective of structural functionalism, the dual-income families and single-mother families common among marginalized races and in the lower classes were "dysfunctional," thus inherently inferior to the breadwinner-homemaker family model.

Symbolic Interactionism

The major premise of symbolic interactionism is that social reality is socially constructed and defined through human interaction and the use of symbols, most notably language. While structural functionalism focused on broad macro-level changes that seemed to unfold in an almost mechanistic and inexorable manner, symbolic interactionism offered a micro-level perspective that focused on human agency and social interaction as playing important roles in shaping social life and the world. Symbolic interactionism originated in the work of early nineteenth-century pragmatic philosophers like William James and John Dewey, who saw social structures as dynamic and changeable rather than static and fixed, emphasized human beings as active creators of social reality, and argued that meaning emerged within the context of social interactions (LaRossa and Reitzes 1993; Ingoldsby 2006). One of the early theorists in this field, W. I. Thomas, coined the phrase "definition of the situation" to explain the importance of meanings in shaping reality. In the well-known Thomas Theorem, he declared that "if men define a situation as real, then it is real in its consequences." In symbolic interactionism, even one's sense of self, or social identity, was a product of human interaction.

The basic premises of symbolic interactionism have been widely embraced among scholars since the early 1900s as a way to understand social life, but it was not until 1938 that Herbert Blumer (1969) coined the phrase "symbolic interactionism." Many social thinkers contributed to the development of symbolic interactionism and its many subtheories (e.g., labeling theory, social role theory, the theory of self).

Symbolic Interactionism and Social Inequality

Symbolic interactionism is not often used to theorize social class inequality and does not offer a single, coherent explanation for any dimension of social inequality. Some of the basic premises of symbolic interactionism, however, offer insights into the emergence and consequences of social inequality. For example, one of its basic assumptions is that people live in a physical and symbolic environment, communicating primarily through symbols that have socially constructed meanings. Symbols are used to evaluate people and all aspects of life—whether things are attractive or repulsive, good or bad—and children internalize these evaluations through socialization (Burr, Leigh, Day, and Constantine 1979). Still, because meanings are socially created they can also be socially changed; in fact, one of the great appeals of symbolic interactionism during the era of significant transformation and social change was that it offered people hope of having some control over their lives and the broader society (LaRossa and Reitzes 1993).

Symbolic interactionism holds much potential for understanding how patterns and ideologies of social inequality emerge through social evaluations of difference and for understanding the adverse consequences of social inequality. For example, Max Weber argued that social class inequality cannot simply be understood as based on the distribution of occupations and income; it also includes more subjective factors, such as power and status. There are a variety of ways to win power and status, but inequalities are perpetuated by processes of social consensus among human beings. The power that men had in their families, for example, was legitimized authority based on tradition. Status, or the amount of honor, prestige, or esteem a person has, is also based on social evaluations and definitions. Although dominant groups play a major role in defining who has status, it is also the case that considerable agreement exists among people in the same population with respect to what constitutes high and low-status jobs, lifestyles, and consumption patterns. People who occupy high-status jobs may disdain, belittle, and even stigmatize those in lower-status positions, and the latter are often resentful and hostile about their station in life.

Other concepts that fall under the umbrella of symbolic interactionism also offer valuable insights for studying social inequality and its impact. The *theory of the self*, for example, holds that human beings are reflexive and introspective and, through interaction with other human beings, create definitions of themselves—or self-concepts—that have major consequences for their everyday lives. Those who have a positive self-concept, for example, are likely to have a stronger sense of self-efficacy, higher aspirations, and better overall physical and mental health. Another strand of symbolic interactionism, *labeling theory*, also speaks to the power of symbols (or words) to affect one's sense of self and behavior. Applied primarily to the study of social deviance, it holds that judging and sanctioning those who fail to adhere to socially constructed norms and rules can have devastating consequences, such as producing shame and stigma or creating self-fulfilling prophecies. But although social labeling occurs, people have some latitude in deciding how to respond; for example, they participate in the social construction of reality and can challenge or reject labels.

Symbolic Interactionism and the Family

Some theorists (Ingoldsby, Smith, and Miller 2004) argue that symbolic interactionism has had a greater impact on the field of family sociology than any other theory. Such a claim seems remarkable given the saliency of structural functionalism in family sociology, but it is explained by the fact that much actual empirical research on families focused largely on sex roles, a concept that was of key importance in both theoretical traditions. Structural functionalists argued for the efficiency of families that were specialized in their functions and based on distinct sex roles for men and women, and symbolic interactionists focused on how language and communication were essential to the way couples defined and adjusted to their marital roles.

Ernest Burgess has been credited with bringing symbolic interactionism into the study of the family in the 1920s, when he described the family as a "living, changing, growing thing" (LaRossa and Reitzes 1993:158). Burgess argued that modern marriages were based less on legal, formal contracts and more on social factors like companionship, love, and compatibility; thus, marriages were subject to bargaining and negotiation between husbands and wives. Consequently, much of the research on families sought to understand how married couples communicated, resolved marital conflict, and created a common definition of their relationship. This approach to understanding marriage accepted as a reality that marriages were based on love and distinct sex roles for men and women, and, as Lasch (1977:43) contends, research often equated marital success with conformity or adaptation to sex roles, while ignoring the impact of social forces on marital success. Indeed, sex role theory proliferated among symbolic interactionists, although they were more likely than structural functionalists to see sex roles as constantly being negotiated rather than static and to argue that couples had a great deal of latitude in deciding how to prioritize and fulfill social roles. For example, while there are expectations associated with the role of "mother," women exercise some choice in deciding how they will fulfill that role.

Conflict Theory

Conflict theory offers an explicitly critical perspective on social class inequality and the origins and consequences of such inequalities. The roots of the theory date back to the 1500s, but the best known among classical conflict theorists is Karl Marx, a philosopher, socialist, and major critic of capitalism and the emerging industrial economy. Marx noted that industrialization, which began in England in the 1700s, had left millions of workers with no choice other than to enter the exploitative production system, which had been devised by capitalists and which was creating vast differences in the quality of life between workers and business owners. He argued that industrial capitalism had created two diametrically opposed social classes: capitalists (the bourgeoisie) who owned the means of production and laborers (the proletariat) who worked for them. Appalled at the industrial factory system, Marx criticized how workers had been deprived of the tools of production and how technologies were stripping them of their autonomy, creativity, and dignity. With the advent of factories, the division of labor, and the extensive use of new machines and technologies, Marx argued, the nature of work had "lost all individual character, and, consequently, all charm for the workman," rendering the worker "an appendage of the machine" forced to perform "only the most simple, most monotonous, and most easily acquired knack that is required of him" (cited in Grusky and Szelenyi 2006:27).

Marx saw societies as controlled by the ruling class, or capitalists, who exploited workers and whose worldviews shaped the dominant ideologies. But he maintained that social class inequality was neither fair nor inevitable; in fact, Marx argued that the earliest human societies were classless and based on the communal ownership of land and resources. The origin of private property had changed the natural equality that once prevailed in societies, sparking a history of class struggle. The demise of the feudal economy and the accumulation of property had fueled industrial capitalism, which was now supported by the dominant ideologies and state policies (Hurst 2004). But Marx predicted an end to capitalism once class consciousness emerged among workers, which would inevitably occur because of growing misery among workers and the nature of work itself. For Marx, work was both a way for laborers to survive economically and a transformative process in which individuals and societies evolved (Farrington and Chertok 1993:360). He predicted a crisis in capitalism would unfold as a result of overproduction, and intense competition for profit among capitalists would lead to a concentration of misery among workers (e.g., lower wages, more unemployment). Eventually, workers would unite, rebel, and overthrow capitalism, creating a classless society.

Conflict Theory and the Family

Conflict theory provides the most coherent critique of social class inequality in the field of sociology; however, prior to the 1970s it was seen as a missing theory in the study of family studies, or at least a theory that had failed to fulfill its analytical potential (Farrington and Chertok 1993:357). Still, Marx and his cohort, Friedrich Engels, did not completely ignore families; rather, they were very critical of the emerging bourgeoisie family, which they saw as oppressive to women. According to Marx and Engels, gender inequality was the earliest and most basic form of inequality; the dominance of men over women was, in their view, analogous to the dominance of capitalists over workers—both were relationships based on exploitation. A more contemporary critical theorist, Lasch (1977:5), contended that industrial capitalism offered the promise that private life would compensate workers for the harsh, unsatisfying labor they were required to perform, and oppressed women by casting them as "angels of consolation" who would make the family a private refuge. Marx contended that the family should be abolished because it involved the domestic slavery of women (Adams and Steinmetz 1993), a notion that was a far cry from the idealization of love-centered marriages and harmonious family life that was often found in structural functionalism or symbolic interactionism.

Prior to the 1970s, American sociologists, whose ideas were dominant in the field of family sociology in the Western world, thoroughly rejected Marxist theory as reflecting fascism, socialism, and communism (Farrington and Chertok 1993:360–362). Scholars, in fact, saw the family as an ideal representation of the democracy and egalitarianism of American culture (Truxal and Merrill 1947). However, since that time, scholars and social activists have become more willing to embrace the tenets of conflict theory in studying families. In a 1979 article, Jetse Sprey described conflict as a new theory in the study of families. Conflict theorists start with the premise that human beings are inherently self-interested and, given that resources are limited, they operate on the basis of competition. As Sprey explains, social inequality is an inherent feature of social life because there are continuous confrontations within and between societies over scarce resources (Sprey 1979:132). Since marriage is a dyadic relationship based on love, exclusivity, and intense interaction, it is especially subject to conflict (p. 142). Thus, conflict theorists highlight competition, conflict, and bargaining among family members, as well as issues such as the abuse of power in families. During the 1970s, for example, studies of family violence proliferated. Conflict theorists also shed light on the relationship between families and the broader economy.

Theorizing Gender Inequality

Feminist theories of gender inequality are broad, multifaceted, and sometimes in tension with each other (Osmond and Thorne 1993; Lorber 1998). They share, however, a tendency to draw on the premises of symbolic interactionism and conflict theory to explain gender inequality and an allegiance to several central themes. At the core of feminist theories is an emphasis on the domination of women by men (Cherlin 2008:25) and the idea that the patriarchal order has adverse consequences for women. Gender inequality has its origin in the notion that women are inherently inferior to men, which justifies their oppression and subordination. A second unifying theme in feminism is the contention that gender is distinct from biological sex because gender is a socially constructed concept. As Judith Lorber (1998) explains, gender is "a social status and a personal identity, as enacted in parental and work roles and in relationships between women and men," which results when social roles are assigned on the basis of biological sex (p. 7). Historical and cross-cultural scholarship confirms the observation that gender is constructed on the basis of cultural, economic, and political forces. For example, although patriarchy is widespread, the actual degree of gender stratification in societies varies based on several factors, such as the demands of the physical environment, women's contribution to economic production, the emphasis on female fertility, and the nature of kinship structures (Sanday 1981; Chafetz 1999). Even within a single culture, the gender roles and identities of men and women may differ based on their social class and racial positions (P. H. Collins 2004). Thus, gender is not immutable; it is changeable.

A final unifying element of feminist theory is the belief that gender inequality is unfair and should be ended. Indeed, as Linda Gordon points out, feminist theory is "an analysis of women's subordination for the purpose of figuring out how to change it" (cited in Osmond and Thorne 1993:592). Solutions to gender inequality are integrally connected with feminist theories of inequality. Although patriarchy is ancient, the major construction of gender in modern Western societies is arguably the result of industrial capitalism, its separation of family and labor market work, and its exclusion of women from the latter. Industrial capitalism transformed independent laborers into hired workers, and gradually those workers were defined as men. Although as factory workers men lost much of their power as economic actors, they retained their power in families, especially since women and children became dependent on male wage earners for their survival. In this new industrial economy, women were prescribed the role of homemaker and admonished to devote their full-time energies to taking care of their homes and families. Prior to the feminist movement, family studies were dominated by sex role theory and an uncritical acceptance of the idea that families should be characterized by a clear gender division of labor between men and women.

Feminist Theories of the Family and Social Class

Feminists have argued that the family is the very linchpin of gender inequality because it is organized on the basis of distinct "sex roles" for men and women (Risman 1998). They argued, for example, that the concepts of "sex" and "role" are inherently contradictory because sex is biological and roles are social expectations (Osmond and Thorne 1993:601). Many theorized women's family roles in the context of Marxism, pointing out that industrial capitalism and patriarchal ideologies were intersecting forces in the subordination of women (Hartmann [1977] 2005). Although the new family and industrial order called for a public-private split in the responsibilities of men and women, women in essence were being asked to produce and rear children to be future workers, while serving as a reserve army of industrial workers who could be called upon when needed to enter the labor market and could be paid less than men (Lorber 1998). A few radical theorists contended that this arrangement was at the core of women's subordination and annihilation as social entities and that families and biological reproduction should be eliminated (Firestone 1970:16–18). Marxist scholar Shulamith Firestone believed we were on the edge of a technological revolution that would free women from their reproductive roles, their dependence on men and marriage, and their overall oppression in society (pp. 35, 82). Most feminist theory, however, criticized the public-private split in family responsibilities and argued for greater opportunities for women to combine family and economic labor and more equity between men and women in the domestic arena.

Feminists have drawn on and expanded the insights of symbolic interactionism and conflict theory to include gender oppression and have criticized social class theory for virtually ignoring women. Most social class theory has used the family as the basic unit of analysis; however, in essence this has meant focusing exclusively on men because they were seen as the major wage earners. This approach not only ignores and devalues the work women perform in their homes and the labor market but, as Joan Acker (2006) points out, assumes that all women are married. Even critical theorists like Marx and Engels, who argued that the earliest system of oppression was based on sex, ignored the productive labor of women and saw gender stratification as epiphenomena—the result of efforts by male capitalists to protect private property and biological paternity. Despite this criticism, theorists have not been very successful in integrating gender into the analysis of class.

One early effort was to argue that "housewife" should be categorized as an occupation, but it was difficult to theorize or categorize a position that was without clear job requirements or pay and did not lend itself to social mobility. Moreover, it was virtually impossible to describe the housewife role because the work, prestige, and lifestyle of housewives varied greatly depending on the male wage earner. Thus, although most feminists agree that the family and reproductive work of women is essential to the economy and should be counted as work, most of the debates about including women in the class system have subsided (Acker 2006). With women entering the labor market in larger numbers, however, there have been efforts to explore how women define their own social class positions, and the findings support the use of the family as a basic unit of class analysis. Women rarely assign themselves a social class position that is separate from their husband's. Although in the past women derived their status from their husband's occupation and income, those in dual-income families today use a status-sharing model that includes their own and their husband's occupation and income.

An Intersectionality Approach to Gender

Feminists have made a compelling case that gender is a socially created identity, but even more important, a social structure and organizing principle in virtually every society. To some extent, gender transcends social class and color lines because in virtually every area of life—families, politics, the labor market—women as a group have less power, prestige, and authority than men. Still, "woman" is not a homogenous category because women live across the economic and racial spectrum, differ in terms of their histories and life circumstances, and are subject to racially specific expectations and stereotypes. As P. H. Collins (1990) explains, the dominant controlling images used to describe black and white women have differed radically, with white women depicted as innately pure, domestic, and submissive and black women seen as mammies, matriarchs, and Jezebels. Thus, feminist theorizing about families became a point of contention among women, as the dominant critique was inspired primarily by the family ideals and images of middle-class white women and reflected their experiences. As Osmond and Thorne (1993:609) point out, marginalized women, such as lesbians, working-class women, and women of color, were often left out of feminist theories because feminism drew on a concept of family that was ideologically and inherently biased. For example, the public-private split of family responsibility was a class- and race-based concept that assumed marriage and heterosexuality and was primarily applicable to white, middle-class families. Working-class and poor families often could not conform to the male wage-earner family model, nor could many racial and ethnic minority families; in fact, even after slavery ended, African American families were penalized for even attempting to exempt women from the labor force (Jones 1985; Dill 1988). Middle-class African American women arguably pioneered the revolution of women combining labor market and family work (Landry 2000), and low-income and single mothers are urged to work outside the home rather than rely on welfare.

Black women activists during the nineteenth century recognized the necessity of addressing gender inequalities within the context of racial and social class differences. During the 1960s, Frances Beal (1970) revived this idea by describing being black and female as "double jeopardy" because African American women were penalized by racial *and* gender inequalities. Since then, many scholars have argued that race, gender, and social class act together in creating multiple oppressions for women of color (P. H. Collins 1990; Zinn and Dill 1996). Rose Brewer (1993), for example, notes that for African American women, "gender takes on meaning and is embedded institutionally in the context of the racial and class order [and in] productive and social reproductive relations of the economy" (p. 17). Thus, this intersectionality perspective has since become a useful tool for expanding and enriching feminist theories (Crenshaw 1997).

Theorizing Race and Ethnicity

Since the 1500s, contact between white Europeans and people of color on other continents has resulted in efforts to explain racial differences, most often differences between whites and non-whites. European contact with people of color, the racialized Other, tended to reinforce their ethnocentrism because they viewed other cultures as primitive and inferior to their own. But although ethnocentrism is an important precondition for racial and ethnic stratification, as Noel (1968) explains, it is not sufficient for creating social stratification systems. Without the motivations of finding cheap labor, developing land, amassing resources, and creating wealth, ethnocentrism may have resulted in nothing more than studies of different cultures, racial stereotypes, or curiosity about people of color. With competition over scarce resources and differential power, however, it became the basis for economic exploitation and slavery. These practices were rationalized by dominant groups who constructed most people of color as less civilized, less intelligent, less capable, and even less than human. Such thinking played an important role in the economic exploitation and social oppression of racial minorities, including genocidal practices that were sometimes used to control North American Indians and the enslavement of African Americans.

Racial and ethnic diversity has always been one of the chief characteristics of the United States population, and policies for dealing with it have ranged from segregation to assimilation. Most of the classical sociological theories discussed in this chapter devoted little attention to racial/ethnic minorities and their families, although the general tenets of these theories held important implications for such families. Structural functionalism, for example, with its focus on societal evolution and the survival of the fittest, could be used to explain the low socioeconomic attainment of racial minorities. Moreover, the structural functionalist notion that modern families were nuclear in structure (rather than extended) and adhered to the breadwinner-homemaker family model certainly stigmatized African American families. Most theorists embraced these concepts, even the few studying racial and ethnic minority families. For white ethnic minorities, assimilation was the solution: They were to abandon their foreign ways and Americanize. As Peter Kivisto (2002) explains, the melting pot metaphor was a powerful and pervasive ideology from the early nineteenth through the middle of the twentieth century, with campaigns proliferating across the country to erase the cultural heritage of new immigrants and replace it with American attitudes and beliefs (pp. 46–47). But although this was effective for white ethnic groups, the need for cheap labor and the belief that people of color were inherently inferior made it difficult for them to assimilate into mainstream society, although most tried to do so.

To refute racist theories, scholars drew on the tenets of symbolic interactionism and conflict theory. Symbolic interactionism held that race itself was a social construct, rather than a product of biology. Although people of color are placed in large descriptive categories, such as being Native American, Latino/Hispanic, Asian American, or African American, there is significant variation between the people within each racial category. For example, Puerto Ricans and Cubans are both described as Hispanic, but most occupy quite different places in the social class structure and differ in their historic and cultural experiences. Asian Americans come from numerous and diverse nations, and there are literally hundreds of Native American tribes. The diversity in the African American population stems from growing class polarization, racial intermarriage, and more recent immigrants from Africa and the Caribbean. Even "whiteness" is socially constructed and, for many white ethnic groups, an achieved status and an ideology that upholds privilege. Conflict theorists often give an economic rationale for constructing race. In the 1930s, Oliver Cox, an African American Marxist scholar, argued that as an ideology, racism was rooted in the efforts of capitalists to exploit labor, whether using racial minorities as cheap laborers or to divide workers. By the early twenty-first century, more family scholars were using critical race theory to study the impact of racism on families. There are several branches of critical race theory, but they hold in common the view that race is fluid and socially constructed rather than a fixed entity, that race shapes all social organizations (including families), that racism is institutionalized, and that racial stratification is reproduced through racialized systems and social practices (Burton et al. 2010). Consistent with the premises of symbolic interactionism and conflict theory, critical race theory emphasizes the fact that despite our categories, there are no "pure" (or unmixed) races and that racial categories have served as the justification for subordinating and economically exploiting people of color.

Race and Family Theories: The Case of African Americans

Most theorizing concerning families of color focused on African Americans, who until 2000 were not only the largest racial minority in the United States, but were the only population whose families had been shaped by centuries of slavery followed by racial segregation that most stringently enforced the black/white color line. Slavery had controlled the labor and family lives of black people and had also denied them the right to enter legal marriages, encouraged nonmarital childbearing, and often ignored the importance of fathers by defining black families as composed of mothers and their children. The prevailing perspective prior to the 1960s was that slavery and racial segregation had practically destroyed the African culture and black families, resulting in high rates of poverty, marital failure, and single-mother families. Northward migration had also played a role in undermining African American families because many who migrated were unable to find work in the North or send for their families. Scholars studying black families accepted the major theories of the day, such as the value of assimilating into the mainstream culture and creating male-headed, two-parent families. Most also accepted the structural functional paradigm and its contention that isolated nuclear breadwinner-homemaker families fostered economic success and mobility. Thus, single-mother families became the focus of much research on African American families because they were seen as a major source of social pathology and poverty. For example, E. Franklin Frazier (1948), one of the most prominent black scholars of the 1950s, argued that single-mother families were a legacy of slavery and an obstacle to success. He held that although "matriarchal" families often worked well in the rural South, such families were at a disadvantage in urban, industrial areas.

Despite the focus on single-mother families and poverty, Frazier and most other scholars recognized the diversity of blacks and used a social class perspective to study African American families. They were aware and critical of the racial barriers faced by African American families, and the social class perspective helped shift the focus from biology to social factors and enabled them to show the diversity of black families (Frazier 1948). Some scholars, for example, argued that middle-class white and black families were quite similar in their family structure and values (Davis and Havighurst 1946); however, the fact remained that the majority of blacks were poor, and while most struggled to survive and achieve some level of stability, others were unemployed, involved in crime, and/or completely left out of the cultural mainstream. Social class analyses often characterized African Americans based on socioeconomic achievement as well as conformity to dominant cultural values. W. E. B. DuBois, for example, the earliest scholar to describe the black class structure, posited a four-tier model: On the top tier were those in the middle class and above, and on the bottom tier were the "vicious and criminal classes" (Furstenberg 2007:433). Others, undoubtedly as an appeal to racial justice and greater opportunities, detailed the social pathologies of African Americans living in poverty (Clark 1965). In light of the argument that slavery had destroyed the African culture and racism and segregation had precluded blacks from assimilating into the mainstream culture, it became common to describe those who were low income as "culturally deprived."

D. Patrick Moynihan drew on that scholarly literature in his 1965 book *The Negro Family: The Case for National Action*. Moynihan emphasized how slavery had adversely affected African American families, leading to a pervasive pattern of poor, single-mother families that were inherently an obstacle to socioeconomic success. Noting that nearly one-third of all black families were headed by single women, Moynihan contended that single-mother families and the absence of fathers and husbands from families were at the heart of the problem facing African Americans. Issued at the height of the civil rights movement, however, the Moynihan Report became the center of political contention because it was seen as shifting attention from racial segregation and discrimination as the source of the plight of blacks to the weaknesses of their families. In addition, he described their weaknesses primarily as failing to conform to the two-parent nuclear family structure with gendered roles for men and women—a family model that was already being criticized by feminists. His work served as a catalyst for a new genre of scholarship on African American families that rejected the assumed social pathology of poor black families, focused on their cultural strengths and survival, and challenged narrow theories of what constituted a viable family.

For example, a seminal study by Andrew Billingsley (1968) broadened the premises of structural functionalism by arguing that a variety of family structures could be defined as functional for African Americans—dual income, single parent, extended—because of their unique historical experiences.

From Social Class to Culture: Racial Minorities in Family Studies

The social class perspective embraced by scholars prior to the civil rights era had largely denied the significance of biological race or the African culture in shaping black families; in fact, the prevailing wisdom was that slavery had destroyed their African heritage. To some extent, this stance was strategic, to deny notions of inherent racial inferiority and emphasize the ability of African Americans to assimilate into mainstream society. But the 1960s saw what Steinberg (2001) has described as an outbreak of "ethnic fever" sparked by black nationalism and a growing sense of ethnic pride and solidarity among racial/ethnic minorities. This new sense of cultural pride was reflected in work on African American families that sought to refute the idea that their culture had been destroyed by slavery or was inherently pathological. Pivotal works by scholars of the civil rights era, such as Herbert Gutman (1976), emphasized that slaves had developed a culture of their own based on strong family and kinship systems, while others embraced an explicitly Afrocentric perspective that argued that race should be the very center of any analysis of African American families because race and racism were the central factors in promulgating distinctive cultures among people of color (Nobles 1974; Asante 1987). Such theories also rejected the notion of cultural deprivation or pathology among racial/ethnic minority families and began to highlight their strengths (R. B. Hill 1972; Allen 1979). Among the cultural strengths of African American families noted were an emphasis on shared childrearing, extended families, and, to some degree, gender egalitarianism among married couples. Between the 1960s and 1980s, the focus on cultural strengths resulted in a plethora of studies that inadvertently valorized low-income single-mother families by describing them as headed by strong, self-reliant women who were supported by extensive kinship networks (see, e.g., Stack 1974).

This new cultural perspective on families was extended to include other racial minorities, expanding the scope of family studies to include groups hitherto neglected. But to some extent, families of color have similar historical backgrounds (e.g., they came from less-developed nations) and encounter similar circumstances in the United States (e.g., social and

economic marginalization). To the extent that it exists, the cultural unique-
ness of their families typically reflects these factors. For example, based on
their traditions (and often religious beliefs), Mexican Americans marry at
younger ages, have more children, and have more two-parent single-earner
families than other low-income racial minorities. (Cherlin 2008:163).
Similarly, the cultural traditions of Asian Americans include a strong expec-
tation of loyalty and service from children to their parents. But although the
cultural perspective can help us understand racially and ethnically diverse
families, it faces several distinct problems. The first is that marginalized
racial minorities are more similar than different in the strategies they employ
to survive; for example, the cultural traditions of practically every racial/
ethnic minority group emphasize a greater reliance on extended family ties
and respect for the elderly. Such similarities raise the question of the distinction between what is a cultural value and what is mostly an adaptation to
economic factors. Second, cultures are dynamic rather than static; they
change over time. Efforts to link the family practices of racial minorities to
those found in pre-colonial Africa or other less-developed nations can prove
problematic because they ignore social class diversity among blacks and run
the risk of perpetuating racial stereotypes. Moreover, in recent years, it has
become evident that the cultural values or coherent identities shared by
African Americans simply do not transcend generational or social class
boundaries (Hill, Murry, and Anderson 2005).

Among African Americans, the cultural strengths perspective began to
lose its appeal by the 1980s when, despite the creation of equal opportunity
and affirmative action policies, many African American families and communities were worse off than before. Rates of marriage were plummeting
and those of nonmarital childbearing escalating, even as extended family ties
were weakening. Although many qualitative studies continued to endorse a
cultural approach to understanding African American families (Allen 2001;
R. Hill 2001), especially emphasizing their extended families and strategies
of sharing childrearing work, more quantitative and comparative research
reported few, if any, differences in the support systems of black and white
families (Roschelle 1997). Overall, the cultural perspective has lost much of
its currency (McAdoo 1998; Aponte 1999; Sarkisian and Gerstel 2004).
Aponte (1999) argues that although cultural differences are now more celebrated than criticized, they appear to be overstated. Similarly, McAdoo
(1998) notes that the characteristics associated with black culture are mostly
class-based survival strategies that transcend racial categories. In fact, social
class diversity has always characterized black families (Landry 1987; E. J.
Hill 2005; Bowser 2007), and that diversity has increased significantly since
the civil rights era (Wilson 1978). The emphasis on cultural diversity between

families continued to wane in the early twenty-first century, with scholars often noting that relying on traditional cultural markers to explain families is overly simplistic and leads to erroneous conclusions (Burton et al. 2010).

Bringing Social Class Back In

As this chapter has shown, American scholars were slow to embrace social class theory—at least critical or Marxist theory—due largely to the threat of communism, the emphasis on the United States as a middle-class society, and our national focus on socioeconomic mobility. The most popular early theory, structural functionalism, contended that even when social class inequality existed, it was justified by the skills, abilities, and efforts of individuals. During the late 1960s, critical theory became more accepted as the result of the social protest movements, and elements of it were incorporated into theories of racial and gender inequalities. But this often has obfuscated social class inequality, despite its growing intensity and the fact that it makes theorizing women and racial minorities as homogenous entities more difficult. The diversity of women has challenged visions of gender equality since the nineteenth century, when the first wave of feminism was met with a strong antisuffrage movement among women, most of them white and upper class, who felt giving women the right to vote was a threat to the family (Camhi 2007). Racial diversity and racism also undermined the unity of women, often complicated by the fact that women of color often had a broader agenda than white women because they saw the need to fight poverty, unemployment, and racism (Franklin 1997:16).

The second wave of feminism faced similar problems. Osmond and Thorne (1993:606) concede that the notion of "woman" in most feminist research was, "at least tacitly, white, Euro-American, class-privileged, and heterosexual." Modern feminism has always included at least a few women of color, but many African American women have seen feminism as failing to meet their needs and, worse, as simply racist (Ferree and Hess 1994). African American women, for example, often did not view marriage, being a housewife, or motherhood as oppressive and could not relate to the images of white womanhood or female exclusion from the labor market (Dill 1979; Jones 1985; P. H. Collins 1994). In recent decades, with the entry of white women into the labor market, social class differences between women have also become more visible. Women have made many inroads into high-paying, traditionally male occupations in recent years, but most of that progress has been made by educated middle-class women (England 2010). Many scholars have sought to integrate gender into social class theory, but the results have been disappointing. Although the intersectionality perspective has heightened awareness of racial differences in the construction of gender, social class often gets lost because of the implicit equating of white with middle class and black with lower/working class. Some class theorists, in fact, have argued that gender is a separate analytic system that simply cannot be integrated with social class analysis (Wright 1997).

The political unification of African Americans during the civil rights movement and the shift from the social class to the cultural perspective also made it difficult to see growing class divisions among black people. Few scholars seemed willing to confront the issue of the declining quality of life for many African American families in the post–civil rights era, until sociologist William Wilson (1978) documented growing class polarization. Wilson advanced the controversial thesis that the significance of race in the lives of African Americans was declining and that social class differences were increasing and ultimately shaping their life chances. Although educated African Americans were able to make significant gains during and after the civil rights era, increasing the size of the black middle class, the loss of industrial jobs among unskilled black men had produced an urban underclass. Indeed, although Wilson's thesis was and remains controversial, the pattern of social class polarization he documented among blacks was shaping the lives of all Americans.

The social class system in the United States has undergone significant transformations in the past 30 years due to technological, political, and economic changes. The industrial economy dominated during the bulk of the twentieth century, with a proliferation of jobs that often paid decent wages, provided benefits such as health insurance and sick leave, and required no more than a high school education. Yet with technological advances and the rise of the global economy, such jobs had begun to wane by the 1970s.

In the next three chapters, I offer a social class perspective on families, and then I conclude with a chapter that examines families in a changing global economy. Using the lens of social class to analyze family life presents two immediate problems: There is no consensus among sociologists about the definition of social class or on the actual number of social classes that exists. As indicated in Chapter 1, I use Gilbert's (2008) definition of social classes as "groups of families more or less equal in rank and differentiated from other families above or below them with regard to characteristics such as occupation, income, wealth, and prestige" (p. 11). This definition places members of a single family in the same social class and assumes some diversity among people in the same social class position. It also resonates with the tendency among sociologists to define social class as based on multiple factors—occupation, education, and income—which many consider to be a measure of socioeconomic position (Hurst 2004:12).

But the boundaries between social classes are never clear, and clarity diminishes as the number of classes increases. For the purposes of simplicity, I base this analysis on three broad social classes: elite and economically affluent families, middle-class families, and economically marginal families. Regardless of the social class categories one devises, there is no homogeneity in the experiences of families who occupy those categories. One reason is that other factors (e.g., religious beliefs, family structure, political orientation) also affect the nature and quality of family life. Moreover, social classes are not fixed entities; they are dynamic and subject to change based on cultural, economic, and political factors. For example, the distinction between blue-collar and white-collar workers, based on whether an individual did manual or nonmanual labor, was once used to distinguish between the working class and the middle class. With the demise of blue-collar jobs and the deskilling of white-collar positions, that distinction is rarely used today.

3

Elite and Upper-Class Families

In her memoir *Personal History,* Katharine Meyer Graham (1997) traces her family's rise into the upper class to her grandfather, a member of a distinguished family with French Jewish roots dating back many generations. He immigrated to the United States in 1859, as the nation was rapidly industrializing and modernizing. Although his family origins were more than humble, his life story exemplified the American Dream: He worked as a store clerk while learning English, eventually became the owner of that store, and went on to become a wealthy banker. As a result, Katharine's father, Eugene Isaac Meyer, grew up in a privileged family: He graduated from Yale University at the age of 20 and, restless with his progress at a major law firm, began to invest money in real estate and the stock market at a crucial period of economic expansion, eventually buying a seat on the stock exchange. Meyer had already made millions of dollars by the time he met his wife-to-be, Agnes Ernst, a recent graduate of Barnard. Katharine describes her mother as a strikingly beautiful, intelligent young woman who was immersed in the world of art and supporting herself as a freelance writer. Her marriage to Meyer typified that of upper-class couples: She brought to the union beauty, education, and sophistication, while he was a business tycoon who had made a fortune of $40–$60 million by 1915 and was to go on to purchase the *Washington Post.* Meyer's fortune enabled Ernst to continue to pursue her artistic and intellectual interests while making a home for her husband and children.

For Katharine, growing up in a wealthy family meant having nannies and 10–12 domestic servants at her disposal—for example, she writes of having two bells in her room that she could ring for assistance. As a child, she took private dance, music, and French lessons and traveled extensively; in addition, she was taught class-related behaviors, such as a strong respect for tradition and support for cultural organizations. But part of her class socialization was learning that talking about money and wealth in her house was taboo—in fact, thrift was emphasized—and any thought of living a life of idleness or leisure was eschewed. Her parents emphasized to the children that "you couldn't just be a rich kid, that you had to do something, to be engaged in useful, productive work; you shouldn't and couldn't do *nothing*" (K. Graham 1997:52). Indeed, instilling in their children a sense of *noblesse oblige,* the notion that people born of high rank have the responsibility to be kind to or help others, is common among parents in the upper class.

For many upper-class families, this is expressed through charitable giving: In a recent book, Frank (2007:162) notes that philanthropy remains popular and sometimes even a source of competition among members of the upper class. Families with incomes of a million dollars or more donated more than $30 billion to charities in 2003, up from $9 billion in 1995. Such giving adds to the status of the elite and their reputation for generosity in helping others.

Defining the Upper Class

Katharine Graham's experience typifies much of what comes to mind when we think about being wealthy—servants, multiple homes, extensive travel, an elite education, and a lifestyle based on tradition, manners, and social graces. In 1958, E. Digby Baltzell, a sociologist and member of the upper class, offered the following definition of the "upper class concept":

> a group of families, whose members are descendants of successful individuals (elite members) of one, two, three or more generations ago. These families are at the top of the *social class* hierarchy; they are brought up together, are friends, and are intermarried one with another; and finally, they maintain a distinctive style of life and a kind of primary group solidarity which sets them apart from the rest of the population. (Baltzell 1958:7)

Referring to its members as being "successful" and "at the top of the social class hierarchy" evades the issue of exactly how much wealth is owned by the upper class, a topic of much interest and debate among social scientists today. Elaine Leeder (2004:168) points out, for example, that at the very top of the wealth hierarchy are the 420,000 American households that constitute the superrich; they have an average of $8.9 million in wealth. Wealth inequality has always exceeded income inequality, but between 1983 and 1989, the concentration of wealth in the hands of the wealthy spiraled in the United States (Leeder 2004; Perrucci and Wysong 2008; Kerbo 2009). For example, 1 percent of Americans own about 40 percent of all privately held corporate stock (Kerbo 2009:163), while the richest 10 percent of the population owns nearly 80 percent of all real estate and 60 percent of all money in bank accounts (Leeder 2004:167). This concentration of wealth has important implications, such as its impact on democracy and political power. Many scholars point out that people with significant wealth control major aspects of the economy and have the power to influence political ideologies and patterns of voting; they also occupy the highest ranks in the political system and have a major impact on political decision making. For example, the majority of people who are corporate directors of banks and industries are from the upper class, as are most of those in Cabinet positions with the government (Dye 1995; Domhoff 2006). Thus, following Max Weber's lead, many include power and control over the economy in their definition of the upper class (see, e.g., Rossides 1997).

Another notable aspect of Baltzell's definition that has been commented upon by other scholars is the cohesiveness of the upper class; that is, those in the upper class tend to be friends who intermarry and experience a kind of group solidarity. He argued that the upper class resembled a caste system, with family life revolving around a complete set of activities and associations. According to Baltzell:

> Even the most socially secure families . . . place a high value on belonging to the correct clubs and associations and making an appearance at the fashionable balls, dancing assemblies, weddings and funerals; and where their children are concerned, the right summer resorts, dancing classes, schools and colleges, and finally, their daughter's debut, are each and severally of vital importance. (cited in Marger 2008:85)

This suggests that the upper class constitutes a closed society of people who rarely venture beyond their own class in forming friendships and associations. That exclusivity extends to living in select cities and neighborhoods where they are isolated (and protected) from their social class inferiors. Perrucci and Wysong (2008:66–67) contend that while the upper class has always distanced itself from the public and public institutions by establishing exclusive schools, neighborhoods, and clubs, this has now nearly taken the form of class secession. For example, there has been a notable increase in the number of gated communities and elite housing areas that are literally walled off from the surrounding areas. Frank (2007) argues that the newly rich have virtually formed their own country, "Richistan," that has a culture that differs from the old established elite. In another work devoted to understanding the new upper class, David Brooks (2000) describes the emergence of what he calls "Latte Towns"—liberal communities situated in magnificent settings that feature "upscale retailers, gourmet bread stores, handmade furniture outlets, [and] organic grocery stores." Thus, this physical class secession is mirrored by the participation of upper-class families in specific activities, elite clubs, and a distinct culture.

Notable in early definitions of the upper class, such as those proffered by Baltzell (1958), is that they include those who are the descendants of economic elites or successful people. This captures the traditional distinction made by sociologists between the upper upper class and lower upper class, or basically those with "old" money and those with "new" money. The highest status is accorded to those with old money, especially the upper upper class that has had wealth for generations, often dating back to the eighteenth century. For them, wealth is inherited and associated with good breeding, social graces, and Ivy League educations—and a strong prohibition against the "ostentatious display and conspicuous consumption" that was once common during the Gilded Age (Mayer and Buckley 1970). Those in the lower upper class have "new money," and while they may be wealthier than those in the upper upper class, most have earned their money in their own lifetime. They typically do not have the well-known family names of the older upper class (e.g., DuPont, Rockefeller) and may lack their cultural habitus and social graces. Thus, despite their wealth, they are set apart from those in the older upper class; for example, as one upper-class woman explained when describing members of the old upper class: "[The old families] will always look at me as an outsider. They've already gone with the same people, and they talk about people I don't know. Their lives are ingrown" (Ostrander 1984:24).

How one earns money and the lifestyle one cultivates are important factors in membership in the upper class. For new money to become a part of the upper class is a process; for example, although John D. Rockefeller earned a fortune in oil in the late 1800s, he was seen as a "gangster" and a social inferior in many upper-class circles (Kerbo 2009). Even today, there are notable status differences and fissures between old and new wealth, although over time they became quite similar in lifestyle. Most live in large homes staffed by domestic servants and own multiple homes. Upper-class children attend "finishing" and "prep" schools and prestigious colleges, where they are expected to cultivate their artistic and intellectual interests.

Birthright is essential, as "ancestry, heritage, and breeding" are major elements in their sense of being upper class (Ostrander 1984). They disproportionately influence the economy and political system and engage in leisure activities that are not easily imitated by those in the lower classes, such as polo and yachting. They spend a great deal of money on travel and philanthropy, and overall they emphasize conservative social attitudes; cultivated tastes in art, music, and literature; and unobtrusive manners (Mayer and Buckley 1970; Kendall 2002).

Finally, being in the upper class has been almost synonymous with being male and white. Marital endogamy has meant that women in the upper class marry men of their own background, so their lives and identities are subsumed under that of their husbands. In recent decades, however, many women have ascended the corporate hierarchy and garnered power and wealth. One study found that the number of corporate directorships held by women grew from 9.5 percent in 1995 to 13.6 percent in 2003, and nearly 90 percent of Fortune 500 companies have at least one woman director (Zweigenhaft and Domhoff 2007). Little research, however, has been done on how this affects marriage and family life.

Whether there was historically—or is currently—an African American upper class is a matter of some debate (Bowser 2007), although there were clearly those who were at the top of the black social class hierarchy and considered themselves members of an elite class. Being considered a member of the black elite was initially strongly related to having light skin and white ancestry; in the late nineteenth century, most were entrepreneurs (e.g., barbers, tailors, grocers), and a few were doctors and lawyers (Meier and Lewis 1959). Black elites worked hard to embrace the same values as their white counterparts. In a study of Boston's black upper class, Cromwell (1994) found that prior to the 1960s, most of them eschewed discussions of race as a problem, emphasized racial progress, refused to associate with anything African, and because interracial marriages were legal in Boston, often married outside their race.

In this chapter, I trace the origins of the upper class in the United States and discuss how their social class position influences family patterns, such as marriage, gender relations, and the socialization of children. My definition of the upper class includes that top 20 percent of the population that can be considered the privileged class, a concept used by Perrucci and Wysong (2008:29–30) to describe that small segment of the population known as the *superclass* (who own immense wealth and control the economy and political system), together with the highly paid managers and professionals who are employed by the government, corporations, and universities. Members of the elite class discussed in this chapter include the "old money" upper class as well as highly educated professionals and successful entrepreneurs, whose increased numbers have caused recent growth in the privileged class. Brooks (2003) calls the new upper class culture the "Bobo Establishment" because its members combine bourgeois and bohemian cultures. The new upper class had its origins in the 1960s, a revolutionary era when intelligence began to compete with heredity as the criteria for entering elite universities. Concerned that they were creating an intellectual aristocracy based on heredity, many universities eliminated Jewish quotas and restrictions on female students, and the number of college-educated Americans skyrocketed between 1955 and 1974. The number of institutions of higher education also increased, along with the number of and need for upper-level professionals. By the mid-1990s, college graduates were earning 70 percent more than high school graduates, and those with graduate degrees were earning 90 percent more (p. 166). Similarly, in *Richistan*, Frank (2007:1–2) notes that the number of millionaire households in the United States more than doubled between 1995 and 2003, to 8 million. Yet, scholarship on family patterns among the upper class has remained relatively scarce as they are often less accessible to researchers. Thus, I draw on a few scholarly works and biographies to explore their lives.

Economic Elites: Historic Origins

The land and resources available for acquisition and economic development in North America starting in the 1600s truly made the continent a land of opportunity for early European settlers. The origins of the upper class in America can be traced to the wealth accumulated by Southern plantation owners and eastern economic elites from the 1700s through the mid-1800s, and then from the emergence of industrial magnates during the late 1800s and early 1900s. In the earlier historical period, agriculture production and the use of slave labor accounted for much of the wealth accumulated by those living in the South, and that wealth typically amounted to several hundred thousand dollars. For example, when George Washington died in 1799, his estate was valued at $530,000 and he was seen as one of the richest Americans in his time. An economic elite also emerged on the east coast based on banking, commerce, and factory labor, and their lifestyles of power and privilege were in stark contrast to those of the masses of struggling workers. Howard Zinn ([1980] 2003) describes New York as resembling a feudal kingdom as early as 1689, when despite widespread suffering and starvation, the governor of the colony bestowed three-fourths of the land to 30 people. Such inequality in wealth also emerged early in Boston where, by

1770, 44 percent of the wealth was owned by the top 1 percent of property owners (pp. 47–48).

By the early 1800s, this hierarchy of wealth had become institutionalized. In the 1840s, for example, there were 39 millionaires in New York and Massachusetts (Mills 1956), and Boston had emerged as the financial center of the world. Oliver Wendell Holmes called members of this upper class "Boston Brahmins" and described them culturally as being noted for their "monopoly on Beacon Hill, their ancestral portraits and Chinese porcelains, humanitarianism, Unitarian faith in the march of the mind, Yankee shrewdness, and New England exclusiveness" (in T. H. O'Connor, 2006:17). Still, upper-class Bostonians eschewed the notion that their identity was based on their wealth and sought to make their city a model of moral and intellectual superiority. As Levine (1980) explains, they were considered the elites of the nation and defined their social status by social graces, philanthropy, education, and religion and only secondly by their business endeavors.

The Industrial Elite

Both the agricultural elite and the eastern elite were challenged by the emergence of an industrial elite and the staggering amount of wealth it amassed. In *The Power Elite,* C. Wright Mills (1956) described the process by which late nineteenth-century business tycoons, often strongly criticized "robber barons," were transformed into economic heroes of the corporate world. During the Gilded Age that followed the Civil War, the opportunities for making a fortune in industry were unparalleled, according to Mills, as the new industrialists had seemingly unlimited natural resources, no military neighbors to oppose them, an ideology of power and progress, and a willing work force. The wealth to be earned from technologies such as the railroad, oil, and steel was further enhanced by the creation of a banking system, the rise of corporations, and a government that favored trusts and was highly influenced by free market principles (Frank 2007:38). In his critical appraisal of the Gilded Age, Mills (1956) writes that the "American elite entered modern history as a virtually unopposed bourgeoisie. No national bourgeoisie, before or since, had such opportunities and advantages" (p. 12). He also notes that economic elites gained their wealth by exploiting resources and workers, killing competitors, and drawing private capital from public sources—all the while using state legislators and lawyers to do their bidding. The emerging industrial economy offered unprecedented opportunities for some to accrue fortunes that far exceeded what was available in the agricultural society. The biggest fortunes in the mid-1800s, according to Frank (2007:38), were between $10 and $20 million, but by the turn of the twentieth century, that had risen to $200 to $300 million. By the early 1900s, John D. Rockefeller, who founded Standard Oil, owned more than a billion dollars in wealth and represented a new historical force in American society (Hall 1992).

Sociologist Max Weber saw Protestantism as a major ideological force in the accumulation of wealth in the United States, arguing that as a religious ideology, it fostered the virtues of hard work and thrift and saw worldly success as evidence of being among God's chosen. Indeed, many industrialists who made fortunes mediated the tension between democratic ideals and unparalleled economic inequality by initiating traditions of personal thrift and charitable giving to educational, health, and welfare organizations. They embraced what was known as the gospel of wealth, which contended that a chosen few had been selected by God to administer the nation's resources in rational ways that would advance the good for all of society (Hall 1992). For example, Andrew Carnegie (1900), a railroad tycoon, wrote that it was the duty of wealthy men to "set an example of modest, unostentatious living" and to "consider all surplus revenues which come to him simply as trust funds, which he is called upon to administer . . . to produce the most beneficial results for the community" (p. 15).

While there were commonalities in their political and economic ideologies, the eastern merchants often disparaged the new industrialists ascending into their class as vulgar, poorly educated, and morally unfit (Beckert 2001). They also feared the rise of industrialization and the loss of their power and wealth to immigrants and other *nouveaux riches*. Many fought to keep immigrants out of the country and to ban those in the country from full participation in mainstream American life. According to Levine (1980), the motivation for developing elite boarding schools was often to preserve the upper-class culture and shield their children from both immigrants and the newly rich. Such boarding schools were one element in an array of strategies meant to separate the old established elite from those who had recently acquired riches but lacked the social graces and manners associated with being upper class. Other efforts by the old upper class to isolate themselves from their social inferiors included the creation of numerous exclusive social clubs during the 1800s and, by 1887, the *Social Register,* which listed the names of acceptable elite and upper-class families. Families wishing to be listed in the *Social Register* had to submit five letters of reference from families who were already in the *Social Register* and, once listed, could be dropped for being involved in scandalous behavior, such as divorcing (Kerbo 2009:158).

Despite efforts by the established upper class to isolate themselves from their newer counterparts, the two tiers have merged over time to form a national upper class. The boarding schools initially established to exclude the *nouveaux riches* gradually came to admit them—often in order to survive economically (Levine 1980). At the height of its popularity in 1925, the *Social Register* was published in 25 cites. In 1976, it was taken over by Malcolm Forbes and consolidated and now includes the names of both segments of the upper class (Kerbo 2009:158– 159). But while members of the upper class now attend the same schools and participate in the same activities, events, and clubs, elements of the fissure between old and new money remain. As the authors of *Class Matters* point out, while the old upper class still eschews the ostentatious display of wealth, many members of the new "hyper-rich" seem to embrace the ethic "If you've got it, flaunt it" (Correspondents 2005). Thus, members of the established elite are not beyond trading "barbarian stories" that focus on the outrageous expenditures and lack of manners of their newer members.

Family Life in the Upper Class

Research on upper-class families is relatively sparse, one result of the fact that members of the upper class are secluded from most other Americans because they have few reasons or opportunities to interact with people from other classes. Historically, one of the key characteristics of affluent families has been their role in choosing the marital partners of their children, largely as a strategy for maintaining and perpetuating wealth. It was not unheard of for marriages to be arranged by parents, but in most cases, parental influence was limited to making sure their children associated only with those from the "right" families. The self-segregation of the affluent from others, as seen in their choice of neighborhoods, schools, and leisure activities, often ensures that their children will marry and develop friendships within their social class. In the 1950s, children from upper-class families attended schools like Groton, Andover, Exeter, and St. Paul's and engaged in elite sports such as fox hunting and polo (Brooks 2000). Cookson and Persell (1985:73) have described the school curriculum at elite boarding schools as classical and conservative. It originally focused on Latin, Greek, rhetoric, and logic and only later included "soft subjects" such as English, math, and history. Children also participated in social debuts as a way of meeting and marrying the right kind of people. As one upper-class mother explained, "The parties are safe. People you don't know can't crash. It's a carefully checked list. You try to match names so you don't get people just off the streets" (Ostrander 1984:87).

In 1975, Blumberg and Paul, replicating a study that was done 25 years earlier, examined marriage announcements from the *New York Times*—considered to be the most prestigious society pages—to study upper-class marriage trends. They found that the names of a significant majority of couples were listed in the *Social Register* and that large, formal marriages at Episcopalian churches were still the norm. Their study revealed how important private schools were as marriage markets: Most of the grooms attended a private school in secondary, if not elementary, school, and enrollment in such schools meant their names were automatically placed on the invitation list to debutante parties, dances, and cotillions. A college education was nearly universal for couples who were marrying, although fewer had attended Ivy League schools than in the past. More recently, Brooks (2000) has argued that the *New York Times* wedding pages have shifted to more of a focus on "genius and geniality" than "noble birth and breeding."

Brides and grooms from the upper class marry at slightly older ages than those in lower social classes, and, although college degrees and career paths are important, there are notable gender differences in education and career aspirations. Grooms were much more likely than brides to have done graduate work (49 percent versus 12 percent), and most men intended to enter traditionally male career paths, such as business or law (Blumberg and Paul 1975). The number of women attending college had increased remarkably since the 1950s, and these *New York Times* announcements emphasized the brides' education and club affiliations. However, no reference was made to future career intentions of brides, which suggested marriage would exempt them from the labor market. Indeed, this gender division of marital labor is evident in research on upper-class couples.

Marital and Gender Relations

The men in upper-class families are often the sole wage earners and perpetuate the status of the family by expanding their wealth, maintaining memberships in exclusive all-male clubs, and mingling with politicians and other economic elites. The upper-class women in Ostrander's (1984) study devoted themselves to being full-time wives and mothers but were also quite involved in philanthropic work. In their relationships with their husbands, many performed what sociologist Jessie Bernard called the "stroking" function of the traditional housewife; that is, they saw their roles as "showing solidarity, giving help, rewarding, agreeing, understanding and passively accepting" (p. 39). As one woman explained:

He's the brain in the family and it's my role to see that he's at his best. I've subjugated everything to that. When he comes home in the evening, this house must be perfectly quiet. I've told everyone the phone must not ring after five o'clock. He wants me to be pleasant, pretty and relaxed. I can't dare cry in front of him or show any emotion. I never bring a problem to him, except during forty-five minutes set aside on Sunday mornings for that purpose. I keep a list. (Ostrander 1984:39)

Ostrander (1984) found that most wives seemed to accept their subordinate family roles and their husband's exemption from domestic affairs. One wife said, "My husband never asks me what I think. He just tells me how it's going to be" (p. 37). Traditional gender ideologies, such as the split between the public and private arena and the notion of the home as a haven and refuge for men, were common:

My husband has never helped around the house or done anything for the children. . . . He expects me to make a nice home to come to, to be a cheery companion, to be ready to go on vacations when he wants to. He expects me to go along with what he wants to do. (P. 39)

It bears pointing out, however, that not all wives are willing to abide by traditional gender and class norms. Ostrander (1984) noted that younger wives and wives who had brought money into the marriage often insisted on more equality in their marriages. Indeed, it is likely that at least some educated, talented women have always challenged this trend, as Katharine Graham (1997) discovered when she read her mother's journal. This journal revealed that Agnes Ernst was determined to marry into wealth, despite having some hesitation about ultimately marrying a man of Jewish ancestry. She saw her marriage, to a large extent, as a business contract that included having children, running the houses, and fulfilling her duty as hostess in exchange for financial support and status. But as one journal entry revealed, she was determined to maintain her own identity and intellectual life:

I . . . rebelled inwardly and outwardly against the suddenly imposed responsibilities of marriage. During the first few years . . . I behaved as if the whole world were in a conspiracy to flatten out my personality and cast me into a universal mold called "woman." So many of my married college friends had renounced their intellectual interests and lost themselves in a routine of diapers, dinners, and smug contentment with life that I was determined this should not happen to me. I wanted a big family, but I also wanted to continue my life as an individual. (P. 19)

Another characteristic common among wives in upper-class families is extensive involvement in community organizations and charity work. Ostrander (1984) attributed this to their very strong class consciousness; they typically understand their class interests and the policies that support them, and they see volunteer work as a way to stave off the growth of the public sector. Their class consciousness was also evident in their clear idea of what it meant to be an upper-class family: They defined it in terms of prominence in their community, being highly respected, having a certain reputation, being well established, and being married to men who headed major business enterprises. Most were aware of their privileged positions, as indicated by one woman who said,

> I was born with a silver spoon in my mouth. I have all the worldly goods that anyone could want. I've never wanted for anything, and I've never envied anybody. (P. 27)

Women in upper-class families play a vital role in displaying and transmitting the proper lifestyle, culture, and social graces through their homes, the servants they hire, and their own style of dressing. They also do the work of keeping up kinship networks, especially among the extended families, which are prevalent among the wealthy and seen as a way of perpetuating their status and class position. In a study of elite Mexican families, Lomnitz and Pérez Lizaur (1987) found that family relations centered on a network of business owners and their wives and children. Women were described as centralizing figures—especially in fostering and strengthening kinship networks in what they called the "grandfamily." Researchers point out that despite their typically subordinate position in their marriages and exemption from the labor force, upper-class women are neither idle nor mere status appendages of their husbands; rather, they are frequently immersed in the world of reform and social activism, participants in cultural events, and members of charitable institutions (Farrell 1993). Their domesticity is in the context of extended family relations and intense sociality that includes business elites and fosters important economic alliances. As feminists have argued is the case for women in general, their lives defy the notion of a tidy division of labor that places men in the public and women in the private sphere of life.

Socializing Children

Social class background is the best predictor of childhood outcomes; it determines how well-adjusted children are, whether they succeed in school and later in the labor market, when and whom they marry, and their ability to create stable families. These outcomes are specifically related to the amount of capital families are able to invest in their children. James Coleman (1988) suggests that there are three types of family capital that affect children: financial capital (income and wealth), human capital (parents' education and its impact on the cognitive environment of children), and social capital (the relationship between children, their parents, and other important family members). These forms of family capital are all related to helping children accumulate "cultural capital," described as an education that focuses on the "best of the west" when it comes to an appreciation of literature, music, social graces, and manners (Cookson and Persell 1985). In all regards, children of the upper class usually fare best.

One of the first things upper-class parents often do to ensure their children's future success is to get them placed in an elite educational setting. Gay, an upper-class mother who was interviewed by Diana Kendall (2002), said she made two telephone calls the moment she learned from her obstetrician that she was pregnant: She called her husband to share the news and an elite private school to place her unborn child's name on their waiting list. Although attending school was several years in the future, Gay explained that she wanted the child to

> learn values that are in keeping with what we try to teach the children at home, and . . . develop playgroups and friendships with other children like themselves, playgroups that help them to know, from an early age, that they will be recognized for their hard work and their personal achievements. (P. 81)

Assembling the right "building blocks" for children was one of the essential childrearing tasks discussed by upper-class mothers, who sometimes referred to their mothering work as creating a "social bubble" made up of the proper environment, educational setting, and friendships for their child's optimal development. As one upper-class mother said,

> We expose the boys to as broad a range of activities as possible, and from that they choose what they're interested in individually. They really have to be very interested in something before we'll support it, but then we'll go all the way with them. (Ostrander 1984:78–79)

Lawrence Otis Graham (1999), who grew up in an elite African American family in the 1960s, interviewed hundreds of upper-class blacks who created their own culture of power and privilege in a nation still segregated by race. Speaking of his own childhood experiences, Graham described his membership in Jack and Jill, an elite organization intended to foster early and high career ambitions among black children. Membership in Jack and Jill is selective and by invitation only, and because the intergenerational transmission of class privilege is more challenging for black elites, the organization focuses on exposing children to a wide range of prominent black professionals. Attending one meeting as a professional role model, he overheard one mother steer her 12-year-old daughter away from her dream of a career in advertising or entertainment by saying,

> Laura needs to be a professional. I'm a professional, her father is a professional, and three of her four grandparents were professionals. . . . She's not going to start her life off by setting us back two generations. (P. 20)

The upper-class women in Ostrander's (1984) study had fairly high rates of fertility and emphasized especially "being there" for their children, organizing their activities around their children's schedules. But they clearly expect schools and other social organizations to aid them in instilling the proper values in their children. Elite educational institutions play an important role in socializing upper-class children, as do clubs, organizations, and activities. Kendall (2002) found elite schools emphasize their efforts to educate the "whole child" and focus on tradition, active and responsible citizenship and leadership, cultivating the individual interests and talents of students, and the importance of alumni and parent activities in the networks students can create.

In some cases, overseeing their socialization can become more important than first-hand involvement, so the social capital that accrues from the quality of the parent-child relationship flounders. Katharine Graham (1997) recalls that she and her siblings lived for several years with their nanny in New York, while their parents resided in Washington despite having children who were aged 2, 4, 6, and a few months old. Upon reading her mother's journal, Graham concluded that "motherhood was not exactly Mother's first priority. She rarely mentioned any one of us children individually. I appear in the diary for the first time by name (or by initial, I should say) in February, 1920, two and a half years after my birth" (p. 27). She continues,

> In all the turmoil of the family and our strange isolation both from our parents and from the outside world, we children were left to bring ourselves up emotionally and intellectually. We were leading lives fraught with ambivalence. It was hard to have an identity. (P. 54)

As noted earlier, many upper-class parents instill in their children a sense of *noblesse oblige,* or the need and responsibility to help others. Honor, duty, service, and loyalty are key values emphasized in many elite boarding schools, and they often take students abroad to live, teach, or work in less advantaged countries (Cookson and Persell 1985). Parents stress that growing up privileged is not enough: They want their children to accomplish on their own and maximize their potential, and they are able to give them the resources they need to do so. They want them to be seen as people who contribute to the community and don't mind "pulling the purse strings" to get conformity from their children. Still, their children have only minimal and highly structured contact with people of other races and social classes, as they learn to perform good deeds from within the confines of the social bubble or under the supervision of responsible adults (Kendall 2002).

People who are wealthy live privileged lives, but wealth does not exempt families from experiencing difficulties and hardships. In fact, it may exert pressure on them to obscure some of those problems:

> You are never to talk about what is wrong in your life, only what was right. You live with the fear that family problems will come out. When I was a young bride and a young mother, the pressure to have things going perfectly was agonizing. (Ostrander 1984:30)

In addition, the childrearing practices of economically privileged parents do not always prepare children for effectively managing their own lives. Nelson Aldrich, a cousin of the Rockefellers, said the parents with old money once handed it over to their children with little advice on how to use it:

> The tradition when I was growing up was that you went to a meeting at the law firm of Choate Hall & Stewart in Boston and the family lawyer would explain the terms of the trust that you were going to live on for the rest of your life and that was it. There was no education. You took the backseat to your advisers and trust experts. It was just madness. We had zero training. (Frank 2007:226)

Although there are some remarkable continuities in the cultures and lifestyles of the upper class (e.g., lavish lifestyles, extensive travel, the emphasis on social graces, the investment in children, education), some of its newest members are challenging those traditions. Robert Frank (2007) argues that one of the major characteristics of the new rich is their diversity. In describing the newly rich, or the "Richistanis," he writes,

> Richistanis like to think of themselves as ordinary people, albeit with extraordinary fortunes. They go out of their way to appear normal. Richistanis wear polo

shirts, casual slacks, and open-collar dress shirts, forsaking the old uniform of monogrammed shirts and suits. . . . Richistanis describe themselves as "down to earth," even as they take off in their private Gulfstreams. (Frank 2007:75–76)

In a similar vein, Brooks (2000) notes that some of the radicals of the 1960s have become a part of the new upper class, and they bring to their new class position a critique of conformity to outmoded traditions such as carefully defined gender roles and elitism. He sees them as meritocrats who define themselves more by their accomplishments than their ancestry; still, they seem to have broadened, rather than challenged, the meaning of being in the upper class.

Conclusion

Although research on upper-class families remains fairly sparse, existing literature does provide notable insights into their marital patterns, gender relations, and childrearing strategies. One observation is the continuity of traditions, despite the evolving composition of those who are members of the elite. For example, despite transformations in the roles of women, boarding school curriculums still assume girls are destined to be wives and mothers and need less mental and career preparation than boys (Cookson and Persell 1985), and women often have subordinate marital roles. Although elite women are often extremely active in volunteer and community work, their lives remain fairly invisible, save stories about their work as fundraisers or hosts of debutante balls (Kendall 2002). A recent article in *The Economist* ("Dancing in the Downturn" 2009) noted that the coming-of-age ritual of debutante balls has survived changing gender roles and the bad economy; they attract numerous college-age women, often wearing dresses that cost several thousand dollars.

The tension among elite agriculturalists, merchants, and industrialists may no longer exist, but there are still status and ideological differences between old and new members of the upper class. The newly rich often entered the upper class via education and meritocracy rather than inheritance and family name, and they have introduced new lifestyles (Brooks 2003; Frank 2007). Early researchers such as Digby Baltzell (1958) favored political and economic dominance by the elite but hoped they would assimilate talented people from less privileged groups, including women and racial minorities. Caste barriers to class mobility weakened during the 1960s and 1970s, but a notable reversal occurred in the following decades, when economic inequality and downward mobility increased, narrowing the opportunity for entry into the upper class.

4

Middle-Class Families

Stability and Change

Most people have a sense of what it means to be middle class, but sociological definitions of the concept have always been a matter of some debate. One reason is that in the United States, the wealthiest nation in the world and one premised on equal opportunity, being middle class was cast as part of being an American. The claim of being a nation of middle-class families also served political purposes during the Cold War era of the 1940s and 1950s, when the economic success of families was heralded as evidence of the superiority of capitalist economies and democracies (May 1999). In one family textbook written during that era, the authors declared that America is a middle-class nation made up of middle-class families, citing as evidence the fact that they *"think alike* on certain broad common problems, no matter what their economic situation, ethnic origin, or social class background" (Truxal and Merrill 1947:23–24, emphasis in original). Thus, being middle class was a matter of having certain attitudes and values. Other social scientists contributed to the ambiguity in defining the middle class by describing it as that vast "amorphous region between poverty and wealth" (Sennett 1974:2). People who are neither wealthy nor poor are likely to see themselves as being in the middle class, even when they are facing economic hardships and challenges. But surveys show that when given the option, many people also define themselves as working class, which carries connotations of having a strong work ethic. Most are reluctant to self-identify as being in the lower class, however, as the concept has behavioral connotations that suggest a lack of adherence to socially acceptable norms (Gans 1995). "Middle class," on the other hand, suggest respectability, upward mobility, and conformity to societal values such as hard work, saving for the future, and getting an education.

From an economic standpoint, the middle class can be defined as those who earn between $25,000 and $100,000 annually—earnings that are above the poverty line but not sufficient to qualify one as wealthy (Marger 2008). In 2005, the median income per household in the United States was about $46,000 (Irwin 2008), which provides a good basis for defining the middle class economically and highlights the fact that being middle class does not exempt families from experiencing financial hardships. But scholars doing empirical research on families often describe those earning up to $200,000 as being in the middle class (Lareau 2002; Seccombe and Warner 2004). As this salary range shows, there are no hard and fast lines for defining the middle class, and those who are in this social class vary greatly in economic resources and lifestyles. For this reason, social scientists often divide the middle class into two groups—the upper middle and the lower middle class—and use income, education, and occupation to differentiate between the two groups.

Members of the upper middle class are usually college educated—many have advanced or professional degrees—and have prestigious, high-level managerial/professional jobs and decision-making power over other workers. Most own property (in most cases a home, but also other forms of wealth, such as real estate, stocks, and bonds). Property ownership is a key factor in middle-class membership; it is a form of wealth and is significantly related to other *life chances,* a term used by Max Weber to describe one's likelihood of having a full and rewarding life. Elmelech (2008:4–5), for example, finds that property ownership is associated with higher levels of physical health, lower mortality, higher self-esteem, more social networks, and more participation in voluntary associations. This more affluent sector of the middle class is distinguished from those in the lower middle class by their education, accumulation of wealth, and consumption patterns.

Members of the lower middle class usually have a high school education and may have additional vocational or academic training, in some cases even a four-year college degree. But generally speaking, their educational attainments are lower and they have occupations that provide less status, power, and wealth. Lower middle-class families are often referred to as "working families" because they rely solely on wages, rather than income from other sources of wealth (e.g., investments). Elementary and high school teachers are typically in this category, as are nurses, firefighters, secretaries, police officers, civil servants, and many others. Those in the lower middle class bring to the labor market important skills and often have jobs that offer stable employment, good pay, and benefits. Middle-class African Americans often fall into the lower middle class; for example, they are overrepresented among those working in lower-paying white-collar jobs and in the public sector (which usually pays less than the private sector). Although many middle-class blacks have left the inner city, they face housing discrimination and are likely to live in economically marginal or all-black suburban areas where they are exposed to many of the same risks found in poor urban areas, such as crime and substandard schools (Pattillo-McCoy 1999; Lacy 2007). Although progress has been made in closing the racial gap in income, the exclusion of African Americans from the housing market created a substantial and lasting wealth gap between blacks and whites. In 2000, the median household net worth for whites was $79,400, compared to $7,500 for African Americans (Elmelech 2008:120).

Despite differences in education, income, and wealth, members of the upper and lower middle class hold many values in common, such as home ownership, financial security, suburban living, adherence to mainstream cultural values, and an emphasis on upward mobility. Although many of those in the upper middle class benefitted from being born into middle-class families, for others, being middle class is the culmination of hard work and social mobility. In her autobiography *An American Story*, Debra Dickerson (2000) describes her parents as Southern sharecroppers who were a part of the great migration northward in the early 1900s, when African Americans usually found themselves almost destined for lives as domestic servants and manual laborers. Eager to escape that fate, Debra spent more than a decade in the Air Force, which enabled her to attend college; she then earned a law degree from Harvard and became a writer. Dickerson describes herself as literally exhausted from the struggle to escape what seemed to be her destiny, as she writes, "The effort of dragging myself from the working class to the middle class, though successful, had nearly killed me" (p. 140).

In this chapter, I examine the development of middle-class families within the context of an industrializing economy that provided new opportunities to achieve a better standard of living and sparked new marital ideologies and childrearing patterns. Overall, industrialization had a modernizing and liberating effect on families. Despite ideologies that prescribed different and unequal roles for men and women, the emphasis on romantic love, free choice, and companionship in marriage grew, and couples became less likely to tolerate unsatisfying relations. The individuality, personhood, and proper development of children became more important; for example, children were more likely to be found in schools than factories and less likely to be subjected to harsh childrearing practices. The current economic transition, the rise of the information and services economy, has resulted in the creation of dual-income families and strengthened the ideology of individualism, inadvertently making marriage more optional and fragile. Among dual-earner, middle-class families, renegotiating gender roles and dealing with the competing demands of work and family have become major issues. We start, however, by placing the rise of the middle class in historical perspective.

Origins of the Middle Class

The creation of the middle class dates back to the Renaissance in Europe during the 1500s, when cities and commerce began to expand, opening opportunities to establish wealth outside the agricultural economy (Ingoldsby 2006). In Europe, capitalist markets and industrialization challenged the traditional social class divide between the wealthy, landowning aristocracy and poor peasants by expanding industrial opportunities and initiating a labor wage economy. Industrialization was a double-edged sword in that it led to the decline of the agricultural economy, the loss of many farms and plantations, and the exploitation of factory wage laborers, but over time, it eventually improved the lives of those living in Western societies, spawning the rise of a new middle class. This new middle class of hired wage laborers joined the small business owners, merchants, artisans, mechanics, and others who were middle class, independently employed, and not displaced by industrialization.

The prospects for developing a new middle class were even stronger in the United States because it lacked a history of feudalism and monarchy and championed the ideology of an open and equal society. It developed the earliest and strongest middle class in history, with property-owning farmers, entrepreneurs, and independent craftsmen prominent from the nation's origins (Bowser 2007; Marger 2008). Despite the growing accumulation of wealth in the hands of a few, the development of this "middle" group helped diffuse class warfare between the rich and the poor, as small planters, farmers, and merchants—even those who were struggling economically—were skillfully included in the rhetoric of liberty, property, and citizenship (Zinn [1980] 2003). By the 1840s, while the nation was in the throes of an economic transformation from agriculture to industry, the United States was described by Alexis de Tocqueville as being closer to equality in wealth, mental endowments, and power than any country in the world or recorded history (Kerbo 2009). Themes of equality, opportunity, and economic mobility through hard work symbolized the American Dream, despite the existence of persistent and institutionalized social inequalities based on gender, race, and social class. Such inequalities were often minimized but never really ignored. As discussed in Chapter 1, they were the subject of critiques by social theorists and spawned social protest throughout the nation's history—from slave and worker rebellions to the civil rights and women's protest movements of the twentieth century.

The rise—and especially resilience—of a strong middle class challenged Karl Marx's critique of industrial capitalism, as he posited the evolution of a two-tier class system in which capitalist owners and workers were increasingly polarized, leading to a revolution. Although Marx recognized the existence of the middle class, he saw it as a transitory class and insignificant as a historical agent of change. He focused on the millions of workers who were stripped of meaningful work and the ownership of the tools of their own labor and forced to take on demeaning, low-wage, and often hazardous factory jobs in order to survive. Such exploitation was, indeed, prevalent, but workers in capitalist nations (some with the direct help of Marx) organized labor unions and won concessions from owners. And although communist unions did exist in the United States—and gained significant strength during the Great Depression of the 1930s—most American workers favored unions that bargained for greater worker benefits within the capitalist system, rather than those that proposed an overthrow of the system (Hurst 2004). Moreover, as capitalist industries grew and became too large to be managed by their owners, a new managerial middle class of workers emerged who had higher wages and good employee benefits. By the 1920s, the transition from competitive to monopoly capitalism and the birth of the corporation created a plethora of well-paying white-collar professional and managerial jobs, in most cases filled by people who aligned themselves with owners and often became stockholders in the corporations that employed them. The rise of the middle class stood as a testimony that one could achieve the American Dream through persistence and hard work.

The Modern Middle-Class Family

The American middle-class family had two distinct incarnations in the twentieth century, described here as the *modern family,* which grew out of industrialization, and the *postmodern family,* spawned by the current information and services economy. As noted in Chapter 1, the rise of the modern middle-class family in the United States came about in the late 1800s, although it is deeply rooted in economic changes that began in Western societies much earlier. For families, it specifically meant the exclusion of women from the paid labor force and the *doctrine of separate spheres,* a gender ideology that held men should be the sole wage earners in families and women should devote their time to taking care of the children and performing domestic labor. This breadwinner-homemaker family ideology was enhanced by the ability of men—mostly white men who held unionized or professional jobs—to earn a *family wage* from their employers: a wage sufficient to care for dependent wives and children. New gender ideologies reinforced the importance of women being in the home; for example, the *cult of true womanhood* defined women as having four cardinal virtues that were intrinsic to their nature: piety, purity, submissiveness, and domesticity (Zinn and Eitzen 2002:64). These prescriptive attributes became standards for women to live up to as they channeled their energy into making their homes a refuge of love and affection for their husbands and children.

Homemaking itself took on the aura of science, with girls trained in high schools in the arts of sewing and cooking, but the work of women in the home was especially elevated by the discovery of childhood as an important and crucial stage in life. The old philosophy of children as born sinners was replaced with the notion that they were born amoral and asocial and needed intense attention to develop properly. As noted earlier, the modern family brought with it new ideologies about children, including the idea that women should have fewer children but invest more emotionally and psychologically in the rearing of those children. Fertility rates declined with industrialization due to improved methods of birth control, more educational and economic opportunities for women, and the fact that children were no longer economic assets because their labor was not needed to help support the family. Instead, children were redefined as the emotional assets of their mothers, who were expected to devote considerable energy to their care.

The modern family was also based on a modern marriage, one entered into on the basis of romantic love and sustained by companionship and marital satisfaction. Despite the emphasis on male authority and specific gender roles for men and women in families, modernization strengthened ideologies of individualism, freedom, and equality in marital relationships, with the tradition of marriages based on patriarchal domination, religion, and procreation gradually giving way to the idea that marriage should be based on free choice, romantic love, and gender equality. Sociologists Burgess and Locke (1953) characterized these changes as "the rise of the companionate marriage," emphasizing that married couples were companions who fulfilled each other's emotional and sexual needs. This focus on marital happiness resulted in less tolerance for marriages that failed to live up to these new expectations, and the divorce rate more than tripled between the late 1860s and 1910 (Cherlin 1992). Still, this family ideology was a reality primarily for white, middle-class families who had the resources to conform to the breadwinner-homemaker family model. Only after World War II did this family model become available to the masses of Americans, and even then, large segments of the racial minority population remained in poverty and low-paying, low-skilled jobs.

The Golden Age of the Family

The breadwinner-homemaker family ideology reached its zenith in the 1950s, which by some accounts was the golden age of the family. This family model had been idealized for nearly a century, but it took the economic affluence of the post-war economy to make it attainable for the majority. During this era, the fervor to reunite and strengthen families was heightened by the deprivations experienced by millions during the Great Depression, the staggering loss of life during World War II, and a revitalized economy that enabled families to realize an unprecedented level of economic prosperity. Early marriage, the birth of the baby boom generation, and suburban living epitomized the family ethic of the 1950s: Couples married younger, and between 1940 and 1957 the fertility rate rose 50 percent (Kline 2001). With the advent of television, shows like *Ozzie and Harriet* and *Leave It to Beaver* characterized the American family as a white, middle-class, suburban, gendered entity in which men and women had clearly defined roles and responsibilities. Family historian Stephanie Coontz (2005) explains that during the postwar era, the "cultural consensus that everyone should marry and form a male breadwinner family was like a steamroller that crushed every alternative view" (p. 229).

It was also the postwar economic affluence of the late 1940s and 1950s that solidified the notion of America as a middle-class society. Martin Marger (2008) identifies two factors that, from an economic standpoint, account for the phenomenal growth of the American economy. First, the United States was the only advanced nation with its economy still in place. Substantial investment by the corporate sector in manufacturing plants and high rates of unionization resulted in thousands of new industrial jobs (Coontz 2007; Perrucci and Wysong 2008). Second, during the Cold War the military industrial complex expanded exponentially, which kept millions of workers employed making weapons. The federal government also played a major role in establishing male breadwinner families and a middle-class living standard by heavily subsidizing educational and housing benefits for veterans. Coontz (2007:75) points out that of the young men starting families after World War II, 40 percent were eligible for such benefits. Thus, the rate of home ownership increased from 43.6 percent in 1940 to 61.9 percent in 1960, due largely to the robust economy and federal lending for housing through the GI Bill of Rights (Elmelech 2008). But the family model of the 1950s was also infused with politics: Not only was its success heralded as a victory of capitalism over communism, but the successful suburban family was seen as a buffer against labor unrest, social class warfare, and the threat of nuclear attack that would especially devastate crowded cities (May 1999).

The federal policies and employment practices of the 1940s and 1950s have been described as an "affirmative action program for whites" (Royce 2009) because racist policies and restrictive lending practices prevented many African Americans from fully enjoying the benefits of the new prosperity. Still, they experienced economic and social mobility during the era. As Bart Landry (1987) explains, prior to this era, the black middle class was restricted to light-skinned biracial children, most of whom were the heirs of white slave owners and enslaved women and who directly served the African American community as teachers, clergy, doctors, and lawyers. But migration northward and greater opportunities resulted in a second iteration of the African American middle class based more on achievement. In 1949, the income for African Americans, adjusted for family size, was about one-third of that for whites but, as Dalton Conley (1999) explains, it had increased by 173 percent (versus only 110 percent for whites) by 1969. Although this median income was still less than half of that earned by whites, by 1964, 9 percent of African Americans (compared to nearly 25 percent of whites) had moved into professional or managerial jobs. Based on a definition of middle class as households whose income was twice the poverty line, the percentage of African American households that moved into the middle class rose from 1 percent in 1940 to 39 percent in 1970. Black women, especially, experienced occupational mobility: In 1940, nearly 60 percent held domestic work jobs, but that figure declined to 6 percent by 1980, as black women moved into clerical jobs (Pattillo-McCoy 1999).

Postmodern Middle-Class Families

In many ways, the middle-class family of the 1950s was a culmination of the ideological and economic transitions that had begun in the late 1800s and were fortified by the post-war prosperity. Although there were real and even unprecedented economic gains during this era, the idealization of the traditional family of the 1950s obscured a host of problems and underlying tensions families faced during that era (Coontz 1992), while also ignoring the transitory nature of the breadwinner-homemaker family structure. Within two decades, the economy was evolving from industry to information and services, undermining the high wages of male breadwinners and creating a proliferation of traditionally female-typed jobs (e.g., clerical work) that drew women into the labor market. The rise of a post-industrial economy coincided with the rise of postmodern families. *Postmodern* can be defined in several ways, but I use it to describe the growing diversity of families (e.g., the surge in divorces, single-parent families, same-sex couples), growing challenges to the traditional definition of the family, and the fact that families no longer follow predictable life course trajectories.

One of the key characteristics of the postmodern family has been the entry of women into the labor market, and thus the rise of dual-income families. This has often intensified the family and marital trends that began in the nineteenth century, such as the decline in patriarchal and hierarchical relationships and an increased emphasis on marriages based on gender equality, sexual fulfillment, and emotional satisfaction. As Andrew Cherlin (2004) argues, marriage has been deinstitutionalized: It has made the transition from being an institution based on social norms, religion, laws, and gender roles meant to control sexuality, reproduction, and labor to a social relationship based on affection, love, and emotional satisfaction. The entry of women into the labor market and delayed marriage and childbearing have fostered greater independence and made marriages more optional and fragile.

Most Americans still plan or hope to marry, but middle-class couples are more likely to be able to do so than poor and low-income couples. Middle-class couples, freer than in the past from pursuing marriage as a strategy of economic survival or compliance with social norms, are even more likely today to emphasize the importance of marrying for love. Paul Amato and his associates (2007), for example, report that male and female college students in the 1930s ranked love fourth and fifth (respectively) in importance in considering a marriage partner, but today both rank love as number one. Anthony Giddens (1992) argues that the focus on romantic love creates a more individualistic perspective on marriage, one in which personal feelings and emotional attachments to specific others take precedence over the customs and traditions that once governed marriage and family life. Increased individualism has fostered what Giddens refers to as the "pure relationship"—a relationship based on autonomy, love, reflexivity, and continual negotiation—and which lasts only as long as it is beneficial to both partners.

Love-based marriages are inherently less stable than marriages based on tradition and clearly defined roles and responsibilities. Developing long-term relationships is not particularly compatible with an emphasis on individualism, independence, and personal happiness. In addition, the investments required for a long-term relationship increasingly compete in a marketplace filled with opportunities for instant intimacy. The sexual revolution, effective birth control, and greater acceptance of nonmarital sexuality and childbearing have strengthened the market for short-term intimate relationships. Moreover, although most men and women would like to marry, gender still shapes marital and sexual ideologies, as men remain better able to separate romantic and passionate love and focus on the latter, without social sanction or penalty. Women, on the other hand, tend to seek long-term commitments and marriage, at least partially because of their desire for a stable and secure environment in which to have and rear children. But despite their greater interest in marriage, women experience less marital satisfaction than their male partners.

In the 1970s, sociologist Jessie Bernard ([1972] 1982) described gender differences in marital satisfaction by arguing that within each marriage there were two marriages: his marriage and her marriage. Bernard argued that husbands generally had happier marriages than their wives because women tended to lose their identity and independence in marriages that were organized around male prerogatives. Some of the gender gap in marital satisfaction is likely due to the fact that women are simply more relationship oriented than men and often invest more effort in trying to create relationships based on good communication, harmony, and cooperation. Wives make more adjustments in marriage than husbands (Bernard [1972] 1982), engage in more emotional work to shape and monitor their feelings (Hochschild 1983), and do more of the "marital work" required to sustain a relationship (Hackstaff 2004). Their greater tendency to give (rather than receive) support and nurturance is seen in the fact that they derive fewer health benefits from marriage than their partners (Waite and Gallagher 2000). In a study that looked at changes in marital satisfaction over a 20-year period from 1980 until 2000, Amato et al. (2007) found that wives scored lower than husbands on five dimensions of marital satisfaction: Wives were less happy and more prone to thinking about divorce than were husbands, and they reported less interaction, more conflict, and more problems in their marriage. Still, they found gender differences in marital satisfaction were not as great as they had been in the past.

Renegotiating Family Work

The doctrine of separate spheres that made men responsible for wage earning and women for family work has become less tenable in the postmodern era, in which the majority of married women, including those with young children, are employed. The entry of white middle-class women into the labor market represents a breakdown of the breadwinner-homemaker gender bargain, which has been challenged by both economic and ideological forces. The growth of dual-income families fostered greater ideological support among men and women for gender equality in families, but this support has seldom been met with an equitable distribution of power, child care, and household labor. In 2007, 76 percent of all married women with school-aged children were in the workforce and, although women do less housework than in the past and men help more, equity in the domestic arena has remained elusive. Most middle-class, college-educated couples believe men and women should be equal partners in marriage. But although men acknowledge the logic and fairness of gender equity in the domestic arena, there is little to suggest that they were dissatisfied with traditional male privileges or saw greater involvement in the domestic arena as a gain. In fact, research shows that when couples share housework, marital satisfaction increases for women but actually decreases for men (Cherlin 2010b).

Hochschild (1989) describes the inability of wives to negotiate an equitable division of "second shift" labor, despite their labor market participation, as the "stalled revolution," and has shown how the frustration of wives takes a toll on marital happiness. When women are engaged in labor market work and are still responsible for most of the housework, there is a significant leisure gap between husbands and wives, with wives complaining of having much less time for rest, relaxation, and hobbies. In one study, a wife who was asked whether she had any hobbies responded this way:

> Actually, no. At this point, I don't. I used to like to paint, but I don't have the time to paint anymore. I really don't feel like I have the time to do much of anything anymore. . . . [My husband's] got lots of hobbies. He's got plenty of time to do it all. (Tichenor 2005:44)

Having the responsibility for both labor market and family work has led many women to experience their marriages not only as unfair, but as a relationship in which the costs outweigh the benefits. Research has not consistently found that employment increases the risk of marital separation or divorce, but it clearly gives women more options and leveraging power.

The origin—and especially the persistence—of gender inequality in the domestic arena has been the focus of several theories. To some extent, childbearing and childrearing tie women to the domestic arena, as did patriarchal family ideologies that transformed biological differences between men and women into specific gender roles. Some theories have focused on gender socialization: Families simply socialize daughters—either explicitly or by modeling gender behaviors—to assume the responsibility for housework and the care of children. Others, like economists, have invoked rational choice theory to explain the gender division of labor: They suggest the gender division of labor makes sense because men have more earning power than women and thus should invest in labor market work while women invest in the care of families. Earlier sociologists often relied on a resource theory to explain gender inequality: Spouses who bring the most resources into the family (generally the highest wages) have the most power, including the power to exempt themselves from housework. This theory, however, does not explain why women with significant earnings still perform most of the housework.

Noting that in 2003, 25 percent of all wives in dual-income families earned more than their husbands, Veronica Tichenor (2005) designed a study to find out whether wives with significantly more economic resources (who earned more) than their husbands still did most of the housework. Her study found little support for the resource theory of household labor: Most of the women who earned higher wages than their husbands still did most of the housework. One explanation that emerged was simply that couples feel uncomfortable when gender conventions are transgressed because such transgressions tend to have an adverse impact on marital satisfaction. For example, some wives admitted that they expected their husbands to earn more than they did and criticized their husbands' inability to do so as a lack of motivation. One wife confessed,

> I'm mad that Vince isn't making more money. He's accused me of being mad in the past, and I denied it, but now I see that it was true. I'm especially mad that he hasn't worked harder at finding another job. (P. 158)

Even when women earned more money than their husbands, there was a tendency to want to create an illusion of male control in the family, perhaps to protect the self-esteem of men who were less successful in the labor market than their spouses and preserve the gender order. Despite earning more, wives liked to think of their husbands as providers, as illustrated by a wife who said,

> I'd probably say he was the provider. I don't know why I'd say that . . . actually, I guess because I felt at one time I didn't work, and he did bring home more. Although . . . I do bring home more money than he does, but, um, so I don't know why I should've said that he's the provider. He probably likes to think of himself as the provider. (Tichenor 2005:130)

The tenacity of the gender division of labor in the household may reflect the fact that "doing gender" is ingrained and easy, but as Sullivan (2006) finds, intimate interactions are constantly (if gradually) being renegotiated due to the demands of the economy and greater participation by women in the public arena. For example, these demands have historically made combining paid and domestic work a tradition for African American women, and the result has been greater (although not equitable) participation in the domestic area by black men (S. Hill 2005). Since 1980, there has been a global movement away from gender traditions and a gradual increase in men's participation in household labor.

Balancing Work and Family: Beyond the Housework Dilemma

Feminist scholars have challenged the doctrine of separate spheres, or the divide between the public and private arenas, on many levels, including showing that rather than being distinct spheres, family and work are mutually influential. Family concerns affect work experiences, and the nature, quality, and demands of paid work affect families. Rosabeth Kanter (1977) delineates several ways in which paid work and family life intersect. One influence is how absorbing the occupation is, that is, whether it is an occupational identity and set of responsibilities that are shed at the end of the work day, or whether the job defines the individual and influences family life outside the workplace. Highly paid middle-class professionals such as medical doctors and CEOs have time-consuming jobs and identities that are defined by their occupations, and in some cases, they experience a significant merging of family and work life. Their identities shape the expectations they have of their families; for example, their spouses may be expected to engage in activities, such as charity work or entertaining, that enhance their careers. The time demands of employment may drain workers of the time they need to participate adequately in family life, and the emotional climate and level of stress at work can also take a toll on family life.

A recent study reported that a majority of men (59.8 percent) and women (55.5 percent) experience conflict in balancing work, personal life, and family (Jacobs and Gerson 2004). E. Jeffrey Hill (2005) reports that successful work-to-family facilitation is related to both job and life satisfaction, while its absence is related to heightened levels of stress. But there may also be some gender differences in the impact of these forces as, despite these stresses, working fathers reported more marital, family, and life satisfaction than did working mothers.

The entry of women into the labor market and the growth of dual-earner families has resulted in the demand for more "family friendly" employer policies, or social policies that acknowledge the challenges employees face in reconciling the demands of family life and work. The United States, sometimes known as the "reluctant welfare state," has been slower than other Western industrial nations to enact policies that help dual-earner couples meet the demands of work and family. There is a liberal/conservative political divide on what kind of policies should be enacted. Conservatives are more likely to see family policies as burdensome for employers and interfering with free market enterprises; they are also more likely to endorse gender traditions and prioritize the role of "mother" for women. Political liberals, on the other hand, are more likely to support gender equality in the labor market, day care, livable wages, and broad definitions of families (e.g., same-sex couples, cohabiting couples). Although both liberals and conservatives endorse policies that they believe support families, they differ in their definitions of the kind of support that should be offered. Thus, when policies are enacted—such as the 1992 Family Leave Act mandating employers with more than 50 employees to provide 12 weeks of unpaid leave after childbirth or to deal with family emergencies—they are likely to meet with criticism from both sides of the political divide. However, even though there is little federal legislation supporting working families, some employers are offering support such as flexible working hours and day care centers.

Although policies supporting working families are important, even in nations with generous or advanced social welfare systems gender proves to be a powerful structural inequality that yields only marginally and gradually to policy innovations. For example, the persistence of a gender division of labor is even seen in nations like Sweden, where generous welfare policies seemingly provide the ideal context for more egalitarian family relationships. Numerous studies have shown that Swedish fathers continue to hold the position of primary wage earner in their families: Few share domestic work equally with their partners, and only a minority (17 percent in 2003) take advantage of parental leave policies (Plantin 2007). The primary reason given is that men are more likely than women to have earnings that exceed the wage ceiling of parental insurance policies, causing the family to lose wages if leave is taken. As one mother of three explained, "We agreed we couldn't afford [his parental leave]. We are already living 'on the limit' every month and could simply not take any more heavy expenses. We lose enough money on my parental leave every month" (p. 102).

Having and Rearing Children

Social class especially influences the decisions couples make to have children, their perceptions of the meaning of parenthood, and the way they rear their children. Middle-class, college-educated women have their first child at a later age than do lower-class women, and 93 percent of college-educated women are married when their first child is born, compared to 39 percent of those who do not have a high school degree (Kennedy and Bumpass 2008). Their pattern of delaying marriage and later onset of childbearing also means that middle-class women usually have fewer unplanned or unintended births and fewer children. Their attitudes about having children may also differ. Some studies show that middle-class parents are more likely than less economically affluent parents to see parenthood as transformative, rather than a routine part of life. One study, for example, found that working-class men saw fatherhood as a natural part of their life trajectory; as one working-class father explained,

> So, when we felt we had done what we were supposed to, both having a job, the natural thing was to have kids. To become Dad was not a strange feeling. It felt just right. You don't have to make a big deal out of this parenting thing. . . . You just have to give it your best. (Plantin 2007:105)

Conversely, a middle-class father said,

> I cannot actually claim to be the same person today as I was before I had kids. . . . I had to reconsider a lot of things in life and in some manner learn all over. You cannot run your own race when you have kids in need of your support. (Plantin 2007:105)

These changes in parental attitudes and socialization strategies emerged from the rise of modernization, industrialization, and the discovery of childhood as a unique stage of life; although, as noted earlier, the treatment of children in colonial America remains a matter of some debate. Research has shown, however, that class differences in childrearing have always existed. In the late 1800s, poor and working-class parents were often seen as overly permissive in feeding, supervising, weaning, and toilet training their children, while middle-class parents were seen as more restrictive and rigid in their childrearing practices. But by the 1950s, an era of social class mobility, there seemed to be a reversal in these class-based childrearing practices (Mayer and Buckley 1970). While lower-income and working-class parents focused on obedience, respect, control, and physical punishment in rearing their children, middle-class parents became more permissive and began to emphasize characteristics like self-direction, autonomy, verbal expressiveness, and creativity (Kohn 1963; Alwin 1984). In a series of studies conducted in the 1950s, Kohn (1963) found middle-class parents were more likely than working-class parents to use reason and psychological punishment in rearing their children. Kohn explained these class differences in childrearing by noting that middle-class mothers read more books and relied more on the experts. Even more important, however, was the fact that parents' childrearing patterns were increasingly shaped by their occupations; that is, middle-class jobs were more likely to require self-direction and working-class jobs were more likely to emphasize conformity to rules, leading parents to rely on class-based values in rearing their children.

The economic and social diversity characteristic of middle-class families has now resulted in a variety of living circumstances for children and childrearing practices, but there is still strong evidence of important social class differences. In the mid-1960s, Baumrind (1966) developed a parenting typology based on the extent to which parents were responsive in meeting the emotional needs of their children and/or demanding and controlling in the expectations they had for their children and willing to use discipline to enforce those expectations. Two of the parenting styles she identified were the *authoritative* parenting style (strong emotional support and moderate social control) and the *authoritarian* parenting style (very strict discipline and little emotional support). She found that middle-class parents were more likely to be authoritative and working-class parents were more likely to be authoritarian. This class distinction in parenting style still holds true as a general rule—middle-class parents are more likely than their working- or lower-class peers to reward their children, attend to and gratify their emotional needs, and use bilateral techniques (e.g., consulting, explaining, negotiating) in interacting with their children. In a study of middle-income and low-income African American families, I found the same pattern of parenting (S. Hill 1999). Middle-class African American parents were more likely to define their role as being a teacher and guide for their children than were lower-income parents, and those with more education relied less on physical punishment in disciplining their children. Even when middle-class black parents endorsed spanking as a strategy for controlling their children's behavior, they spoke of it as being the last resort and generally found few reasons to spank. One middle-class African American mother, asked how she disciplined her 12-year-old son, said,

> Say he did something he wasn't supposed to do. First, we sit down and talk about it and say why it was right or why it was wrong. I want him to understand what he actually did. Once we get past that, we say, "What do you think we should do about this?" . . . I hardly ever spank, ever, even when they were little. Because to me . . . when a parent spanks, they are almost at their last end—they've lost control. (P. 68)

Researchers typically argue that authoritative parenting, most typical in middle-income families, is best for producing socially competent children.

Still, there is some evidence that this might not apply across racial or ethnic lines because culture shapes not only parenting strategies but how they are interpreted by and impact both children and parents. Some research has found racial differences in the impact of spanking on children; for example, spanking was associated with an increase in behavioral problems for white children but not for African American children (Lansford et al. 2004).

Advancing earlier research that often focused narrowly on social class or racial differences in childrearing, Annette Lareau (2002) conducted a study aimed at explicating the social processes by which parents transmit social class attitudes to their children and the implications of those processes. Based on interviews with and observations of parents and their children in a variety of settings and interactive situations, Lareau described the childrearing strategies of middle-class parents as *concerted cultivation* and those of poor and working-class parents as *accomplishment by natural growth*. These childrearing styles are based on how parents organize family life and use language in interacting with their children and on their broader social connections. Characteristic of middle-class parents using concerted cultivation, for example, is family life organized around an extensive set of activities for children—dance lessons, Scouts, sports, music—and an attempt by parents to expose their children to broader cultural traditions than they experienced. As one middle-class African American mother explained,

> I don't see how any kid's adolescence and adulthood could not but be enhanced by an awareness of who Beethoven was. And is that Bach or Mozart? I don't know the difference between the two! I don't know Baroque from Classical—but he does. How can that not be a benefit in later life? I'm convinced that this rich experience will make him a better person, a better citizen, a better husband, a better father—certainly a better student. (P. 754)

Lareau (2002) found that organized activities dominated the lives of middle-class children, often creating frenetic schedules for mothers, and children were unlikely to spend much time at informal play with neighborhood children or with extended family members. Middle-class parents also use language in a way that promotes the reasoning and negotiation skills of their children, often asking their opinions and negotiating with them over issues such as housekeeping, and they teach them to be assertive and outspoken in dealing with professionals such as doctors and teachers. The implication of a middle-class upbringing is that children often grow up feeling special, valuable, and with a strong sense of entitlement.

Middle-class parents emphasize high educational attainment for their children—that they will go to college is often taken for granted—and try to teach their children the value of working for what they have. African

American parents are especially eager to have their children attend college, although those in the lower middle class often fear that their children's attention will be diverted by other popular images of black success. I interviewed one middle-class mother of a 9-year-old son who shared her efforts to shift her son's attention away from being a professional athlete—a goal African American boys are more likely than white boys to have—to focus on becoming a physician:

> He wants to play basketball, but we try to stress right now that he's going to Harvard, and he's going to be a doctor. . . . It's a form of brainwashing, but they need that. And I had a brother who went to Harvard and became a doctor, so he has a good role model. (S. Hill 1999:59)

Gender and Racial Socialization

Social class also affects patterns of gender and racial socialization in families. Families have been seen as key institutions for teaching and perpetuating gender behaviors because they are organized on the basis of gender and explicitly or implicitly teach their children what it means to be female or male. Researchers once found that when parents were asked to describe their new babies, they used words like *strong* and *aggressive* for their sons and *pretty* and *sweet* for their daughters, although other observers who did not know the sex of the child could find no differences between the infants (Leeder 2004:127). In the 1990s, however, Lytton and Romney (1991) analyzed 172 gender socialization studies and concluded that the extent of gender socialization in families is small, nonsignificant, and more likely to be practiced by fathers than mothers. Early research on African American families also claimed that gender mattered little in the socialization of children (Lewis 1975); however, such research often focused on poor single-mother families in which men were absent and all children, regardless of gender, were expected to help out around the house. More recent research on gender socialization in African American families found that social class matters. Low-income parents often hold essentialist notions about their children, especially their sons, and associate any deviance from traditional masculinity as evidence of homosexuality (S. Hill 1999). In general, it appears that middle-class parents—especially mothers—try to avoid teaching their children gendered behaviors (S. Hill 1999; Hertz 2006). But parents face formidable obstacles in doing so when families and other social organizations reflect gender hierarchies. One mother of a son who had just entered kindergarten observed that despite her efforts at an androgynous socialization,

There was this really big thing going on in that classroom around "boys are this and boys are that and we hate girls." And it is the first time I saw this division. I want him to be able to be with both boys and girls and be comfortable. I would like him to be in both worlds comfortably. Maybe there shouldn't be two worlds. (Hertz 2006:180)

Although this mother attempted to avoid exposing her son to gendered behaviors, most parents who challenge gender traditions in rearing their children are more likely to introduce daughters to male-typed activities than sons to female-typed activities, as the feminization of boys often carries the penalty of stigma and disrespect.

Racial Socialization

Historically, studies have shown that most African American parents engage in the racial socialization of their children, and during the past two decades, that research has expanded considerably to explore racial socialization among other racial/ethnic minority groups (Burton et al. 2010). Racial socialization practices are rooted in the belief that children of color are especially likely to be seen as inferior, to be socially isolated from their peers, or to experience discrimination. Middle-class parents are more likely than those in the lower and working classes to explicitly racially socialize their children. Being a member of a racial minority group is often seen as a mark of inferiority, and parents, especially parents with children who grow up in interracial environments, are aware that their children may be subjected to racist comments or stereotypes. Participation in interracial environments explains why middle-class African American parents are more likely than lower-income parents to believe that race may adversely affect their children's futures and to report that their children have experienced a racial incident (S. Hill 1999).

Racial socialization is defined as preparing children for the realities of being a racial minority and includes taking special care to instill in children positive self-esteem (Taylor, Chatters, Tucker, and Lewis 1990). In practice, racial socialization takes many forms—giving children ethnically distinct names, teaching them about their history, and explaining how to deal with racial incidents they experience. A key issue for African American parents who racially socialize their children is finding a balance between enabling them to accept the reality of racial discrimination but still avoiding using race as an excuse for not succeeding in life. As one mother of a 12-year-old son said,

I like for children to know their culture, as far as their roots, our history, but I don't want them to dwell on that. . . . I know prejudice is out there, and

I told the children that prejudice is out there, but don't use prejudice as an excuse. I try to teach my kids how to react . . . to be prepared [for racism] to have some kind of ammunition. And that's where their education comes in, to have something to go forward with. (S. Hill 1999:95)

Beyond preparing children for the prospect of encountering racial discrimination and trying to teach them to succeed despite those barriers, racial socialization can extend to the cultural values children are taught, although those values often reflect class as much as racial differences. Appreciating status differences based on age remains a common ideal in African American communities. For example, when asked to describe the most important values she is trying to teach her children, one mother said, "To respect older people and that she has to realize that she cannot talk to adults the same way she talks to her friends, no matter who the adult is" (S. Hill 1999:56).

Although the research on racial socialization has expanded during the past two decades and studies of "whiteness" have increased, there are few studies of how white parents racially socialize their children. Thus, as Burton and her colleagues (2010) point out, we still know little about how white identity is established or what socialization processes lead white children to embrace discriminatory or nondiscriminatory behaviors.

The Decline of the Middle Class

Although being middle class, regardless of its various definitions, has been a defining feature of successful American families, the rise of the post-industrial economy and the global labor market and the growing impact of technologies have taken a great toll on the middle class. No matter how the middle class is measured, it was clearly in decline in the United States by the 1970s. For example, wages rose steadily from the 1950s until 1973 when, in relation to the rate of inflation, they began to fall, and downward mobility has become more common (Perrucci and Wysong 2008). Wages have increased since then only for the college educated; for example, a male college graduate earned 36 percent more than a high school graduate in 1980 but nearly 80 percent more in 2005 (Marger 2008). There has been a decline in wages in other Western countries as well, but not as much as in the United States. The hourly wages of workers in Germany is 60 percent higher than in the United States, and wages in Sweden are 50 percent higher (Marger 2008).

The strains experienced by middle-class American families—even those earning well above the median household income—have been widely documented in the media and scholarly studies. Even families in the upper middle class—who earn significantly more than the median household wage—have faced strains in maintaining the family's lifestyle. For example, an article in the *New York Times* by Louis Uchitelle (2000) noted that 75 percent of middle-class families earn less than $75,000 a year, and 45 percent of all families earn between $30,000 and $75,000. Although they can usually put food on the table, pay the mortgage, own a car or two, and take a modest vacation, they are increasingly stressed in meeting other expenses, such as "new clothes, child care, lessons for children, restaurants, movies, home decoration, computers, big-screen television sets, stereo systems, Christmas gifts, and saving for college and retirement." Middle-class families at the lower end of the earnings spectrum face direr prospects: They are often unable to meet unexpected expenses such as car repairs, rely heavily on credit cards, and in some cases have significantly increased the number of hours they work each week.

Government policies have also contributed to the declining financial solvency of many families, especially those whose position in the middle class was already fragile. New tax policies favoring the wealthy meant that the top 1 percent of American households captured two-thirds of the increase in national income that occurred between 2001 and 2007, while most other workers experienced wage declines or stagnation and high unemployment rates (Edin and Kissane 2010). The deregulation of the lending industry that began in the late 1990s encouraged families to borrow money beyond their ability to repay, leading to an explosion of debt. Warren and Tyagi (2003) have described how laws and policies that once restricted the ability of middle-class families to borrow money beyond their ability to pay (such as requiring tax returns, credit references, paycheck stubs) were set aside. As a result, families increased their debt loads, overloaded themselves with high-limit credit cards, and purchased homes that required little or no down payment, often at high interest rates, from subprime lenders who preyed on people who could not afford other loans. For example, Warren and Tyagi point out that in the past, most home loans were for 80 percent of the value of the house, requiring borrowers to make a 20 percent down payment to purchase a home, but in the 1990s, the average down payment fell to 3 to 5 percent—despite a clear relationship between small down payments and defaults on home loans. These authors cite research showing that consumers who make a down payment of 5 percent or less are 15 to 20 times more likely to default on their loans than those who put 20 percent down on their homes (p. 133). Payday loans and instant credit, often accessed at exorbitant interest rates, have become prevalent and clear pitfalls for many families struggling to make ends meet. Warren and Tyagi note that in a single year, American families receive more than five billion preapproved credit card offers—more than $350,000 of credit per family—which accounts for the fact that credit card debt increased 6,000 percent between 1968 and 2000. But they note that 87 percent of consumer bankruptcy is due to job loss, medical problems, and divorce/separation (p. 81). And while the middle class has suffered, bank profits have more than tripled since 1970, growing by more than $50 billion.

Key features of growing inequality in the United States have been the distancing of the upper class from the middle class and the decoupling of productivity and wages; for example, although worker productivity rose 16.6 percent between 2000 and 2005, the median household income for families fell 2.3 percent (Irwin 2008:137). Many couples are working longer hours, yet they are still struggling to pay their bills and are experiencing greater anxiety over the prospect of losing their jobs because of the changing economy. For other families, finding stable employment at all is a problem, and establishing married couple families seems remote. These poor and economically marginal families are the topic of the next chapter.

5

Economically Marginal Families

Living on the Edge

The dominant discourse of the United States as a wealthy nation composed mostly of middle-class families often obscures the reality that millions of people in the United States experience substantial economic hardship and poverty. The American Dream was realized by most Europeans who immigrated to the United States in the nineteenth century and achieved economic mobility as a result of hard work. But that hard work paid off because of the burgeoning industrial economy that led to structural mobility, or mobility based on economic and technological change (Gilbert 2003:146). Moreover, for many immigrants, practically any economic stability was an improvement over the circumstances in the countries they had left. Those who worked on farms, mills, mines, or factories considered themselves the working class, but often mostly because they were employed. In *Domestic Revolutions*, Mintz and Kellogg (1988:84–85) document the economic hardships and dire living conditions faced by early industrial workers, including long hours, gruesome work, and wages that fell below definitions of a subsistence budget. Despite this exploitation, workers benefited from the fact that the class structure was still in the making and thus flexible, assimilation was encouraged, and the nation was a world leader in embracing universal education (Esping-Anderson 2007).

Nevertheless, early industrial working-class families lacked the resources to conform to emerging gender and family ideologies that placed women in the home and men in the labor market, and their children—some as young as 10 years old—were often in the labor force (Cherlin 2008:50). Moreover, there was no steady upward ascent: Their economic fortunes waxed and waned throughout the late nineteenth and early twentieth century with the vagaries of the capitalist market, which reached a crucial low during the Great Depression of the 1930s and created joblessness and poverty for millions of people. It was within this context that the official recognition of poverty—poverty not related to the unwillingness or inability of people to work—was born. With the passage of the Social Security Act in 1935, the United States officially became a welfare state that focused on aiding unemployed workers, single women with children, and the elderly. This program expanded sharply during the 1960s with the extension of health care benefits to the poor and elderly, but by the 1990s it was being radically curtailed.

Who Are the Economically Marginal?

This chapter focuses on the family lives of those who are living in poverty and those who live at the margins of poverty. The official definition of poverty is socially constructed based on income, assets, and family size. The current formula was devised in 1955 and is based on the minimum cost of food for families of various sizes. The formula assumes that the average family spends about one-third of its post-tax income on food; the estimated cost of food is then multiplied by three to determine who is poor (Roosa et al. 2005). In 2008, the poverty threshold for a family of four (two adults and two children under age 18) was $22,025; for a family of three, $17,163; and for a family of two, $14,051. Based on this definition, in 2008 about 39.8 million people, or 13.2 percent of all Americans and nearly 20 percent of children, were poor (U.S. Census Bureau 2009). But there is much debate over how poverty is socially and politically defined, with many arguing that these family incomes understate the extent of serious economic hardship experienced by many families. For example, consider the fact that a family of four earning $22,500 a year is not counted among the poor because it earns just a few hundred dollars more than the official poverty line. Absolute definitions of poverty also ignore the different degrees of poverty; for example, 41 percent of the poor live in severe poverty because they earn less than one-half the poverty threshold (Roosa et al. 2005). As we will see in this chapter, poverty is associated with an array of adverse life circumstances, such as substandard housing, high rates of mental and physical illness, inadequate schooling, domestic violence, and poor nutrition. Food insecurity, or not having enough food at all times for active, healthy living, is common in poor families (Seccombe 2007).

Although nearly 40 million Americans are poor, poverty is not randomly distributed in the population; rather, it tends to parallel other dimensions of inequality, such as age, race/ethnicity, and gender. The incomes of the elderly have risen in recent decades due to increases in Social Security, better pensions, and Medicare, but although they are better off than in the past, they are likely to live at or just above the poverty line. Most racial minorities, historically marginalized in the labor market and hit especially hard by deindustrialization and the new economy, have higher rates of poverty than European Americans. Hispanics and blacks have lower levels of education, wealth, income, and home ownership than whites. Although the poverty rate in 2008 increased relative to the previous year for all races, it was lower for non-Hispanic whites (8.6 percent) than for Asians (11.8 percent), Hispanics (23.2 percent), and African Americans (24.7 percent; U.S. Census Bureau 2009). Census data also reveal that foreign-born households (newer immigrants) experienced a much sharper decline in their median household income than native-born households. Single women (24.1 percent) are more likely than single men (17.9 percent) to be poor, and single women who head their own families are five times more likely to be poor than married couples (Royce 2009:249).

This chapter also includes those who are in the lower-paid sector of the working class and the *working poor,* a new category of workers that has emerged in the post-industrial economy. Many of those who were displaced from manufacturing jobs have found new jobs, but most often they are jobs that pay less. Many of the working poor earn wages that are below the poverty threshold, and others earn wages that are barely above it (Cherlin 2008:479). The existence of the working poor helps to account for the fact that the poverty rate in 2008 was significantly higher than in 2004 (U.S. Census Bureau 2009), yet many earn just enough to escape official poverty definitions despite having jobs that do not enable them to provide reliably for themselves or their families. They experience considerable economic hardship working in jobs that pay low wages, have few or no benefits, and are subject to occasional layoffs. In addition, by the turn of the twenty-first century, about 23 percent of the entire workforce was part-time or temporary workers, most of whom have no benefits such as health care, paid sick leave, or vacation leave (Cherlin 2008; Perrucci and Wysong 2008).

Lillian Rubin (1994) argues that the working class constitutes the largest social class in the nation and the most invisible. The rhetoric of middle-class

America remains strong, as is evident from the speeches of politicians who promise to protect or improve their fortunes, but we hear less about working-class families. Rubin defines the working class as those who work "at the lower levels of the manufacturing and service sectors of the economy; workers whose education is limited, whose mobility options are severely restricted, and who usually work for an hourly rather than a weekly wage" (p. 30–31). There is considerable diversity in income among those she defines as working class: In her research, working class family annual incomes ranged from $16,500 to $42,000, with an average income of $31,500. One of the characteristics of the working class is that they seldom draw on public assistance, even when their earnings (or lack thereof) make them eligible. And many were hit especially hard by the Reagan-Bush policies of the 1980s and economic restructuring, leading to personal bankruptcies and foreclosures. But unlike their middle-class counterparts, most knew little about how to save any of their assets. One 38-year-old white male laborer with three children thought bankruptcies were for businesses, not ordinary people:

> After the finance people came and took everything away, I found out that I could have gone bankrupt. Maybe if I'd known about it before, we could have saved some things from those damn vultures. But I never found out about it until it was too late. (Rubin 1994:35)

In addition to experiencing economic hardship, the poor and working class are also often victims of demeaning stereotypes. Accepting welfare has always been seen as counter to the American values of hard work, independence, and success. By the 1980s, the idea of the "welfare queen" was especially popularized and was characterized as an African American single mother with several children with multiple fathers, who drove a luxury car and had children for the sake of increasing her welfare check. Traditional stereotypes also depicted members of the white working class (racial minorities were rarely depicted as working class) as intellectually and socially inferior to their more refined middle-class counterparts. These characteristics were displayed in the media by such characters as Archie Bunker (*All in the Family*), Ralph Cramden (*The Honeymooners*), and Roseanne (*Roseanne*); all were uneducated, overweight, openly bigoted, and lacking in social graces. Social science studies have offered contrasting views of the status of working-class members. In *Blue-Collar Aristocrats*, LeMasters (1975) highlighted the economic success of many highly paid working-class men who often earned more than those with white-collar jobs. Alternatively, being working class is associated with performing unskilled, dirty, manual labor and, as shown in the *Hidden Injuries of Class,* can lead to stigma, shame, and resentment among those in the working class (Sennett and Cobb 1972).

Explaining Poverty

Why do wealthy nations persist in having significant numbers of poor citizens? Given the ideology of America as a land of economic opportunity, biological and personal factors once held sway in explaining poverty; that is, poor people were seen as lacking the innate ability, intelligence, or motivation to succeed. During the nineteenth century, minister and Yale-educated lawyer Russell Conwell traveled the country, giving his popular "Acres of Diamonds" lecture more than 5,000 times. Conwell argued that the poor deserved little sympathy because "there is not a poor person in the United States who was not made poor by his own shortcomings" (Zinn [1980] 2003:262). Early social theorists like Herbert Spencer offered a similar theme; he embraced a social Darwinist perspective, which assumed that the poor simply lacked the physical or intellectual wherewithal to survive in the emerging industrial economy (see Chapter 2). Other major sociological theories did not deal explicitly with poverty, although the structural functionalist framework would likely argue that the poor lack human capital. The human capital perspective might explain the growing gap between the incomes of college-educated and other workers. Alternatively, a Marxist or critical theorist would explain poverty in terms of increasing technology and automation, the capitalist exploitation of workers or the need for capitalism to maintain a reserve army of potential low-paid laborers, and an intensifying pursuit of profit. To some extent, these two competing perspectives form the basis of the cultural and structural perspectives that dominate in explaining poverty.

The Culture-Structure Nexus

During the 1950s, Oscar Lewis explored the perpetuation of poverty among Puerto Ricans and advanced a *culture of poverty* thesis to explain it. Lewis argued that decades of economic marginalization and racial exclusion (e.g., structural factors) led people to embrace cultural practices (e.g., behaviors, lifestyles) that, while adaptive to poverty, were inimical to socioeconomic success. Among the cultural behaviors found among the poor were fatalism, a present orientation, an inability to defer gratification, a lack of thrift and savings, and a tendency toward non-marriage and nonmarital childbearing. Although Lewis saw these cultural behaviors as having their origins in structural forces such as discrimination and exclusion, he also argued that the behaviors became ingrained in the cultures of the poor and persisted even when the opportunity structure was changing. Thus, over time, the cultural behaviors of the poor existed independently of any structural barriers; they became a way of life that perpetuated poverty. Despite the fact that Lewis saw an intersection between structural and cultural forces, his culture of poverty thesis eventually became a focus of much criticism. Scholars rejected the culture of poverty thesis because it was seen as blaming the poor for their own poverty (Zinn and Eitzen 2002:142) and because it considered the cultural values of the poor to be pathological, rather than functionally adaptive. (Allen 1978).

During the 1960s and 1970s, scholars came to emphasize the structural forces that had produced poverty, especially racial and gender discrimination. Feminists argued that the relegation of women to the domestic arena and blatantly sexist employment practices explained the prevalence of women in poor-paying jobs. The decline of marriages and the soaring rate of divorce highlighted the economic vulnerability of women: Indeed, evidence of the feminization of poverty included the fact that women without male partners experienced significantly higher rates of poverty. The cause of the poverty had nothing to do with their innate or cultural characteristics, but rather the fact that the labor market was highly stratified by sex and women were concentrated in pink-collar, female-typed jobs. Acker (1990) argues that in an industrial economy, the very conceptualization of *worker* assumes a male wage earner—someone who is free from competing obligations, such as family, and able to devote practically all his energy to his job.

Racism and discrimination were seen as the major reasons for the low socioeconomic attainment of racial minorities, especially African Americans. Slavery and sharecropping had controlled their labor for literally centuries, and even after those economies ended, African Americans were relegated to the lowest-paying jobs. Other racial minorities faced similar structural obstacles; for example, Mexican Americans endured a system of internal colonialism that defined them as agricultural workers who could work on an as-needed basis, often without ever getting the opportunity to establish roots in the nation. Family theorists studying racial minorities emphasized structures of inequality, but rather than completely abandoning the cultural framework, they transformed it into a strengths perspective that focused on how cultural characteristics enhanced the survival of minority families (R. B. Hill 1972; Allen 1978). Even with post-industrial class polarization among African American families, Allen (2001) insists that black families are best seen as culturally distinct and criticizes scholars for depicting them as nothing more than "darkly tinted facsimiles of White families" (p. 131).

Legislation passed during the 1960s and 1970s effectively challenged the legal grounds for race- and sex-based discrimination, and in the ensuing decades, women and racial minorities made significant socioeconomic strides. Yet, women continue to earn only about 77 percent of what men earn and face *statistical discrimination,* a type of discrimination by employers who see them as mothers or potential mothers with family obligations and thus as less reliable workers. Scholars have noted that there is a wage penalty associated with motherhood and that it increases with each additional child (Avellar and Smock 2003). African Americans and other racial minorities also made significant progress after the removal of structural barriers to success, but civil rights laws did not end racism, racial stereotypes, or racial discrimination. White Americans continue to endorse a spate of racial stereotypes about African Americans, and, while supporting equal opportunity, they often resist policies that would effect such opportunity (e.g., affirmative action, school integration). Much of the progress made by African Americans has taken the form of social class polarization; that is, educated, advantaged blacks have been able to move into better-paying positions while the poor have become even poorer. Examining African Americans as a group, one study found that in the post-civil rights era (1976–1985), the effect of race in diminishing career wages and the racial gap in hourly wages actually increased (Cancio, Evans, and Maume 1996). Many scholars argue that the old Jim Crow racism has simply been replaced by a "kinder, gentler, antiblack ideology" (Bobo 2000; Bonilla-Silva 2006).

The Post-Industrial Decline and Resurgence of Culture

The persistent wage gap between most racial minorities and whites has continued and appears exacerbated by changes in the economy. During the 1950s, some economists were predicting the rise of a post-industrial economy that would result in a permanent underclass of workers who would be excluded from the labor market (Gans 1995). The early loss of industrial jobs disproportionately affected young black men, whose rates of joblessness soared along with their rates of crime, homicide, incarceration, drug use, and non-marriage in the late 1960s (Wilson 1978, 1987). African American men are often sporadically employed, but the Center for Labor Market Studies shows that in 2002, 25 percent of all African American men were without work the entire year—twice the rate for white and Hispanic men. Among African American men who had dropped out of high school, 44 percent were idle the entire year (Herbert 2004).

Although theorists have mostly focused on how the post-industrial economy has affected men, Irene Browne (2000) points out that young African American women who head their own families also have been disadvantaged as low-wage jobs moved to suburban areas, and they actually lost earnings when opportunities were expanding for other women. Earnings for African American women started to decline in the 1980s, despite gains in human capital, due to the increase in nonmarital childbearing and decrease in public sector work (Bound and Dresser 1999; Newsome and DoDoo 2006). The loss of wages by African American women and men correlated with a surge in nonmarital childbearing and welfare dependency and reignited theories that blame poverty on biological factors and cultural values. Herrnstein and Murray (1994) (re)advanced the thesis that race correlates with intelligence and determines one's place in the social class structure and that the extension of welfare benefits had caused an erosion of morality and cultural values among the poor (Murray 1984).

W. J. Wilson (2006) continues to proffer a social structural perspective that highlights the impact of the post-industrial economy and documents widespread stereotypes, especially of young black men, and labor market discrimination. But, like Lewis in the 1950s, Wilson recognizes the link between these structural forces and the cultural behaviors of low-income African Americans. For example, he not only relates high rates of violence and criminal activity in inner-city neighborhoods to a loss of jobs, status, and respect among young African American men, but he describes how jobless poverty shapes cultural behaviors. The consequences for African American children who are born into a culture that is not organized around the routine of work are immense. As Wilson explains,

> Regular employment provides the anchor for the spatial and temporal aspects of daily life. It determines where you are going to be and when you are going to be there. In the absence of regular employment, life, including family life, becomes less coherent. Persistent unemployment and irregular employment hinder rational planning in daily life, a necessary condition of adaptation to an industrial economy. (P. 90)

Most social theorists continue to explain poverty in terms of structural factors, especially changes in the labor market and social policies that play an important role in shaping marriage, childbearing, and other family decisions. Some have pointed out that poverty has become a normative experience; for example, one study found that by age 75, half of all Americans and 90 percent of all African Americans will have been poor for at least one year (Rank 2009). But despite the salience of the structural perspective, it has become more difficult to ignore the growing divide between the attitudes and behaviors of the poor and the affluent, especially in terms of their families. These differences include patterns of marriage, childbearing, and family formation among the poor that are seen by some as cultural traits and as likely to increase social inequality (Edin and Kissane 2010).

The Marriage Decline

People of all social classes hold similar attitudes about marriage: Most would like to get married, have children, and enjoy the companionship of a loving and supportive partner. Economic forces, however, shape their willingness to enter into marriage and their timing of marriage, as seen in the fact that marriage and fertility rates fell during the Great Depression but surged in the post-war era of prosperity. The post-industrial economy has played a major role in a pattern of delayed marriage that started in the late 1970s; today, the average age at first marriage for men and women (respectively) is about 27 and 25 years. Cherlin (2008) argues that marriage has become a capstone experience for many couples—an event that takes place after they have started careers and/or finished college. This delay of marriage has resulted in more people being single for longer periods of time. Census data show that in 2005, 100 million Americans aged 15 and older were single, and 49 million households were headed by single men or women (Strong, DeVault, and Cohen 2008).

Singles are, of course, a very diverse group. They include those who are widowed or divorced, never-married people, gays and lesbians who are unable to marry, single parents, and couples living in nonmarital cohabiting unions. The rate of nonmarital cohabitation has increased tenfold since the 1960s and now includes almost 5 million heterosexual and 600,000 same-sex couples. The majority of young people have lived with an intimate partner at least once before marrying, and most marriages are preceded by a period of cohabitation (Avellar and Smock 2005). Although the trend toward singleness is widespread, it is exacerbated among lower working-class and poor people. Currently, nearly 40 percent of all children are born to unmarried mothers. But researchers have found that social class, measured by educational level, predicts a woman's likelihood of giving birth outside marriage. Between 1997 and 2001, 93 percent of college-educated women were married when their first child was born, compared to 57 percent of high school graduates and 39 percent of those who did not complete high school (Kennedy and Bumpass 2008). Moreover, the likelihood of garnering adequate resources for marriage is higher among those in the middle and upper classes than those in the working and lower classes.

Studies show that low-income populations of all races value marriage as much as their affluent counterparts; in fact, some research shows that low-income and poor African Americans—the group least likely to marry—idealize marriage more than white Americans (Harknett and McLanahan 2004; Huston and Melz 2004). As one mother in Robin Jarrett's (1994) study of low-income, never married, welfare-dependent mothers said,

> I think everybody wants to get married. Everybody wants to have somebody to work with them . . . and go through life with. . . . I would like to be married . . . I want to be married. I'm not gonna lie. I really do. (P. 36)

This sentiment was confirmed in the research by Edin and Kefalas (2005), who examined marital decision making among a racially diverse group of low-income women. They found that economically marginal women scarcely differ from their more affluent counterparts in their desire to marry. Moreover, they want the same attributes as other women want in their prospective partners (e.g., fidelity, nonviolence, economic and social support). The difference is that low-income women simply have more difficulty finding men who can or are willing to provide those things; thus, they end up having babies with men who they believe lack the qualities that would make them good husbands and fathers.

Economic factors play a key role in explaining why people who want to marry do not have the opportunity to do so, but it bears noting that cultural factors also play a role. Prior to the 1960s, most families were composed of two parents, regardless of their social class standing (Cherlin 2010a). Some research shows that African Americans were more likely to marry than whites, despite their economic circumstances, and marriage rates were often highest among those with the fewest resources. Of course, in many cases, black couples living together were merely assumed to be married, and numerous factors, such as northward migration and the inability to find work, often made marriages fragile (Franklin 2000; S. Hill 2005). But as social theorists have argued, there is a connection between structural obstacles and cultural behaviors, and there is some evidence of a strong nonmarriage ethos among African Americans. To some extent, among African Americans marriage has never been as strongly institutionalized as the core of the family (Sudarkasa 1996).

This cultural framework sheds light on the high rates of marriage among Mexican Americans, even those who are poor. Although Mexican Americans and African Americans are similar in terms of socioeconomic attainment, the former are more likely to marry and stay married, and they report having happier marriages. This pattern of marriage success despite poverty has been described as the "paradox of Mexican American nuptiality" (Bulanda and Brown 2007). In their comparative study of the two groups, Bulanda and Brown found that African American couples enter marriages with more risk factors that are associated with divorce, such as doing shift work and having children prior to marriage, and they have higher levels of marital disagreement than Mexican American couples. Mexican Americans were as likely as whites to get and stay married, reflecting the traditions of Catholicism as well as a classic assimilation pattern.

Strained Gender Relations

One of the key issues that has historically impaired the ability of economically marginal couples to create enduring marriages is a gender ideology that endorses men as the wage earners and heads of their families and women as dependent domestics. Although working-class and poor couples do marry, they are likely to face hardships that are exacerbated by disappointment in the ability of men to earn adequate wages. Economic realities make it nearly impossible for some low-income couples to live this gender ideology, but in the past they were more likely to embrace traditional ideologies than were middle-class couples (Rubin 1976; S. Hill 2005), creating a significant gap between their marital ideals and lived experiences. I interviewed one working-class, divorced mother of two children who did factory labor for an electronics company, and I asked how she felt about marrying again. Expressing her eagerness to remarry, she described herself as being such a traditional woman that she simply could not understand why no man wanted to marry her:

> I am very marriage minded! I believe in the cooking and the cleaning. . . . I'm an old-fashioned woman, right out of Proverbs 31. I believe in going to the sales and making sure I get the best for my family, fixing breakfast and ironing clothes. I am not a modern woman! (S. Hill 2005:162)

Many people, perhaps especially those who have never had the opportunity to adhere strictly to the traditional gender order, tend to see such roles as a sign of respectability and success and also as supported by religious teachings. Research shows that African American women are more likely than white women to endorse some gender traditions, such as a man's economic responsibility for the family, and are less likely to be happy in marriages when their income exceeds their husbands' income (Furdyna, Tucker, and James 2008). African American couples have been stigmatized as violating gender behaviors deemed necessary for the formation of strong families and marriages. Nothing better captures that than the "black matriarch" stereotype, which depicted African American women as domineering women who dismissed the importance of marriage, men, and sexual morality by having children outside marriage and heading families. The "black matriarch" stereotype has been thoroughly rejected by scholars and is nearly verboten in academic circles, yet it still exists in popular culture (Franklin 2000; P. H. Collins 2004) and is at the center of gender tensions among some African Americans who still believe women are "simply too strong, too independent, and too self-sufficient for their own good or for the good of their relationships" (Franklin 2000).

The gender tensions among working-class couples are exasperated by the fact that the views of women are changing faster than those of men. Rubin (1994) found that in the 1970s, white working-class men and women embraced gender traditions; however, following up on that research in the 1990s, she discovered a dramatic evolution in the gender beliefs of working-class women: They now fully endorsed the idea of equal pay for equal work and expected the men in their families to share more fully in the domestic arena. But the attitudes of working-class men had not changed as much, leaving them feeling embattled at work and at home. The husbands in her study reported doing more housework than ever before, but they did not embrace the idea of sharing equally. They expected to be appreciated for helping out at home; indeed, as one exasperated husband said, "Christ, what does a guy have to do to keep a wife quiet these days? What does she want? It's not like I don't do anything to help her out, but it's never enough" (p. 87).

The insistence by men on having most of the privileges of patriarchy in the home, even when they are unable to provide sufficiently for their families, does not bode well for marriage or marital success. The traditional gender bargain, in which women sacrifice much of their independence and do most of the domestic and child care work in exchange for the economic support, power, and prestige their male partners bring to the relationship, simply is not feasible for working-class and low-income couples. The decline in the wage-earning abilities of men, especially those without a college education, has made them less likely to be able to offer economic security or status to their partners.

Economic factors matter in creating stable marital unions. In exploring marital decision making among low-income single mothers, Kathryn Edin (2000) found that many were not simply concerned about their male partner's current employment status; they were also concerned about his overall prospects for long-term stable employment. Low-income men often move from one marginal position to another, often with significant spells of unemployment. Women have traditionally "married up," or married men with more money and education than they have, and garnered much of their social status from their husbands, which presents a problem for low-income women. The inability of many men to meet that criterion has led some low-income mothers to see motherhood and marriage as quite separate events (Cherlin et al. 2008); they want the love and satisfaction they expect to gain from marriage, but they believe the men in their lives are not up to the responsibilities of marriage and fatherhood (Edin 2000; Edin and Kefalas 2005). Many do not see the point of sacrificing their independence for the meager benefits they might gain from marriage, although they do want their partner involved in the lives of their children (Blum and Deussen 1996). Even then, they tend to restrict their expectations to what the fathers are able to contribute to the care of the children. As one low-income mother explained,

> I don't expect him to buy my baby snowsuits and boots. . . . It's just the thought. When [my son's] birthday comes around, [his father] ain't got to give him a quarter, he ain't got to send him a card. [He] could pick up the phone and wish him a happy birthday. (Jarrett 1994:43)

This again exemplifies the influence of structural forces, in this case economic barriers, in shaping cultural values and expectations. Research shows that despite preferring marriage, a significant majority of low-income mothers do not believe having a child outside marriage is embarrassing or stigmatizing, although most believe a woman should at least be over the age of 20 before becoming a mother (Cherlin et al. 2008). But beyond the economic factors that undermine the potential for successful marriages, low-income women often mistrust the men in their lives, and many are concerned about infidelity and domestic violence.

The Perils of Marriage

The majority of people eventually marry; in fact, economically disadvantaged people with low educational aspirations and strong religious values are overrepresented among that small minority of Americans who marry before the age of 23 (Vecker and Stokes 2008). But the risks associated with marriage, such as marital unhappiness, domestic violence, and divorce, are all exacerbated by poverty and economic marginality. Recent claims linking marriage to being healthier, wealthier, and happier often have not explored how social class and race mediate the benefits of marriage. Still, research has shown that low-income people and some racial minorities, especially African Americans, receive fewer economic and emotional benefits from marriage than those who are white and affluent (Harknett and McLanahan 2004; Furdyna et al. 2008). The inability of low-income and working-class couples to abide by gender traditions, the growing divide between women and men on gender issues, and the struggle to maintain family stability when economic resources are sparse all predict marital dissatisfaction. Unlike middle-class men, who at least give ideological support to gender equality, working-class men resent what they see as escalating demands by their wives to engage them in more housework (Rubin 1994:87–91). And although African American couples were once seen as having rather egalitarian gender behaviors when it came to sharing housework and child care, this claim has been refuted by comparative research. For example, research finds that although black men are more accepting of wives who work outside the home, their employed wives still do most of the child care and housework in the domestic arena (Blee and Tickamyer 1995; John and Shelton 1997).

Financial woes undermine marital happiness and success, as is evident by the fact that social class is a strong predictor of divorce. In their study of divorced African American men, for example, Lawson and Thompson (1999) found financial strain and male unemployment to be the most frequently mentioned causes of divorce, and these factors were associated with wife abuse. One study by Ball and Robbins (1986) reported that being single produced more happiness among African Americans than being married. African American men who were single, divorced, or separated were happier in life than those who were married, and among women, widows had the highest level of satisfaction. A more recent study found that, compared to white women, black women felt they were receiving fewer benefits from being married; they expressed less trust in their spouses and had lower levels of marital well-being (Goodwin 2003).

Since their origin in the 1970s, systematic studies of spousal abuse have show that it affects couples in all walks of life (Straus, Gelles, and Steinmetz 1980; Johnson 1995), but such research might obscure the fact that those who live stressful lives of poverty and hardship are more likely to engage in domestic violence. Intimate partner violence affects 3 to 4 million women a year and is especially risky for women during pregnancy and the postpartum period (Connelley, Newton, Landsverk, and Aarons 2000). Married women are less likely than those who are separated from or cohabit with their male partners to be victimized by abuse, and being in the lower class and having less education is associated with the most severe kinds of intimate partner violence (Cherlin 2010b:352–353). As Cherlin explains, none of this suggests that low-income people are inherently more violent, but it reflects the fact that they experience more frustrations, such as dealing with inadequate resources. Wage earning and work are major sources of masculine identity and power; their absence portends badly for relationships by undermining the position of men in their families. Men who lack the ability to establish masculinity through traditional means, such as economic and social power, often resort to alternative strategies of masculinity, such as violence, hypersexuality, and infidelity (Hill and Zimmerman 1995). Male violence often emerges when the economic power of men is compromised and they lose control over the labor power of women who enter the job market (Breines and Gordon 1983).

Thus, poor and low-income women have the greatest risk of experiencing intimate partner violence, and that trend is heightened by welfare dependency. Ellen K. Scott and her colleagues (2002) found that as many as 60 percent of female welfare recipients have been victims of violence. In her interviews exploring the reluctance of poor women to marry, Edin (2000) found that violence was a major factor: Many of the women she interviewed had been physically abused during their pregnancy, in some cases resulting in miscarriages. Asked about the advantages of being single, one of the women she interviewed said, "Not living with someone there to abuse you. I'm scared of my bills and I'm scared if I get sick, what's going to happen to my kids, but I'm not afraid for my life" (p. 126).

Having and Rearing Children

One of the ways that social class affects childbearing patterns among low-income and poor women is the tendency to have children earlier in life and before getting married. Many low-income women experienced hardship in their families of origin, got marginal educations, and ended up with few career ambitions; thus, having a child becomes an option for entering adulthood and taking on more responsibility. Low-income females are still more likely to have children during their teenage years than other women. Still, the rate of teenage childbearing is no higher than it was in the 1960s; the difference is that in the past, teenagers were more likely to be married when their first child was born. Today, 27 percent of white and 70 percent of black children are born to unmarried women. Not all of these births are, of course, to those in the lower and working class, although they have a higher likelihood of having births outside marriage. And the birth of a child sometimes results in marriage, although it is more likely to do so for whites than blacks and for couples who have sufficient economic resources. Thus, single-parent families are more common among working- and lower-class families, an issue discussed later in this chapter.

Social class has a greater impact on the childrearing strategies in families than does family structure—whether they are headed by single or married parents—or race/ethnicity. As indicated in Chapter 4, studies show that middle- and working-class families embrace different childrearing strategies, although there has been some convergence in these patterns in recent years. The typical class distinction has been that working- and lower-class families lean more toward authoritarian childrearing strategies; that is, they focus on obedience, conformity, parental power, and control of their children and are more likely to engage in physical discipline (Kohn 1963). A more recent study by Annette Lareau (2003:31) reports that these class differences still exist. Lareau describes the childrearing strategies of low-income and poor parents as *accomplishment by natural growth*, as distinct from the *concerted cultivation* strategies of middle-class parents (see Chapter 4). Like their middle-class counterparts, economically disadvantaged parents love and care for their children and want to foster their growth. But rather than being involved in a host of organized activities (often costly in terms of time and money), their children grow up in a much less structured and supervised environment and spend more time hanging out with relatives and peers. Lareau spent many hours interviewing and observing parents across the social class spectrum and discovered important differences in how parents interacted with their children and expected their children to interact with people in authority and social institutions. For example, parents in the working and lower classes used more directives when talking with their children (rather than asking children their opinions or negotiating with them) and instilled in their children a sense of powerlessness when it came to dealing with authority figures. These characteristics, according to Lareau, tend to perpetuate the disadvantage and sense of constraint experienced by children growing up in low-income and poor families.

Lareau's (2003) study strengthens and updates the earlier work of Kohn (1963) and other liberal social scientists who documented the potency of social class in shaping childrearing. In the 1940s and 1950s, scholars held that social class was even more important than race in how children were reared and often pointed to the similarities between black and white middle-class families. Although these scholars often produced stigmatizing portrayals of poor black families, they also noted that lower-middle-class black families worked hard to protect their children from their adverse surroundings and instill in them mainstream, middle-class aspirations such as an education and white-collar jobs. One study comparing black and white families concluded that the "striking thing about this study is that Negro and white middle-class families are so much alike . . . [in terms of] number of children, ages of parents when married, as well as child-rearing practices and expectations from children" (Davis and Havighurst 1946:708).

This denial of the influence of cultural values on childrearing was challenged in the 1960s and 1970s with the emergence of the *culture of strength* perspective on racial and ethnic minority families. Some scholars argued that the cultural heritage of racial minorities shaped how black children were reared. For example, mainstream cultural values such as autonomy, separation, and individualism were seen as less influential in rearing African American children because they were subordinated to cultural values such as unity, cooperation, and interdependence. Using a cultural approach, Janice Hale (1986) argued that African American childrearing practices were rooted in the traditions of West Africa, where social breadth, expressionism, entrusting the care of children to others, and having people interact with numerous relatives are valued. More recent studies have found that the childrearing practices of racial/ethnic minorities may also be shaped by culture; for example, Japanese mothers place a great value on teaching their children to be dependent on their families and developing relationships of interdependence with others (Rothbaum et al. 2007). Moreover, cultural practices that differ from those found in mainstream middle-class society do not necessarily have an adverse impact on children, as they tend to be interpreted in the context of that culture.

Still, it remains difficult to distinguish the childrearing values that result from cultural values from those that result from social class. As Steinberg and others have noted, social disadvantage has a major impact on the values taught to children, and culture becomes reified when it is unhinged from economic and material realities (Steinberg 2001; N. E. Hill et al. 2005). John Ogbu (1981) argues that the socialization of children is organized around teaching cultural competencies that equip children to survive in their own ecological settings. Comparing middle-class whites and urban ghetto blacks, he argues that these cultural competencies differ based on race and reflect social structural factors, such as poverty and discrimination. Yet, there is a tendency to equate race and social class—whites are middle class, blacks are poor—which denies social class diversity across racial lines. Similar to earlier studies, my research finds that social class, especially as measured by education, leads to a convergence in the childrearing practices of African American and white parents (S. Hill 1999).

Life in Single-Mother Families

The growing number of children living with single parents—especially single mothers—has been the topic of numerous research studies. The number of single fathers living with their own children aged 18 and under has skyrocketed since the 1970s; in 2003, there were 2.3 million single fathers rearing their children, making up 18 percent of all single-parent households (Hook and Chalasani 2008). This shows how diverse single-parent families are, which makes it practically impossible to characterize them as a group. Men and women become single parents through a variety of circumstances, such as nonmarital childbearing, divorce, and widowhood. In the 1970s, the surge in the divorce rate was most responsible for the increase in single-mother families among white women, whereas escalating rates of nonmarital childbearing was the key factor among African Americans, Native Americans, and Hispanics.

The quality of life for children in single-mother households varies tremendously, based on factors such as economics, parenting skills, support from kinship networks, and the participation of fathers and male partners in the lives of children. For example, although families headed by single mothers are much more likely to live in poverty than are two-parent families, a significant percentage of single mothers earn decent wages and provide sufficiently for their children. Consider Jackie Brady, a 31-year-old single mother of a 7-year-old son (Jason), whom I interviewed a few years ago. Jackie, an educator who is currently pursuing a master's degree, provides a nice home for herself and Jason and, despite her heavy workload, they manage to spend a lot of time together. Asked to describe Jason, Jackie said,

> He's curious, adventuresome—very adventuresome—somewhat independent. I would say that's because I'm a single parent. . . . A lot of times he has to go along with me to school, like when I was doing the master's program . . . and I have explained to him that this is the situation we're in, and he's really a help to me. He's a hard worker. He's a real sweet little boy, I really love his sweet spirit, always wanting to help . . . and I would say for the most part he's all boy. (S. Hill 1999:13–14)

Single mothers, like Jackie, often provide well for their children and build strong relationships with them. And many single parents are not rearing their children alone; about 40 percent of single parents live in cohabiting relationships, and the majority of single fathers with custody of their children live in households that include other adult women. Some studies suggest there are few differences between married and cohabiting fathers in their engagement with their children (Gibson-Davis 2008). Men who make a commitment to fatherhood and the mothers of their children experience a significantly increased sense of social and psychological well-being (Knoester, Petts, and Eggebeen 2007). Even if they are not living in households with other adults, single parents are often in extended families or have other supportive relationships. Research from the Fragile Families Study has shown that 80 percent of unmarried mothers are in romantic relationships, some with men who are involved in the lives of their children (McLanahan et al. 2003). Other studies show that those relationships are often long term; as one mother explained, "I been with my baby's father for 12 years. We still not married. So maybe one day we might jump the broom or tie the knot or whatever" (Jarrett 1994:39). Despite this diversity in single-parent families, there is a consensus emerging from scholarly research that children in such families experience more disadvantages and adverse outcomes than those living with two married biological parents.

The Well-Being of Children in Single-Parent Families

Despite the fact that many single-parent families are strong and well-functioning entities, most research shows that the single-parent family structure poses more risks to children and is associated with more adverse childhood outcomes. One apparent reason is that parental investments in children—as measured in money, social capital, or time—are simply higher in two-parent families than in single-parent families (Gibson-Davis 2008).

Many low-income single parents receive support from relatives in rearing their children, but so do families with two parents. Economic factors shape the extent of support more than family structure, while ethnicity shapes the type of support people get from their families. For example, one study found that whites receive more gifts and loans, whereas Mexican Americans are more likely to live with or near extended kin and receive more direct help with child care (Sarkisian, Gerena, and Gerstel 2007).

Extended families, once clearly one of the strengths of poor racial/ethnic families, have weakened considerably in recent decades and, have been shown to have both positive and negative effects on children. Among African Americans, extended family relationships traditionally have meant having the aid and support of grandmothers, but several factors have lessened the strength of these bonds. For example, the growing trend toward multipartnered fertility, or having children with more than one male partner, reduces the support single fathers and mothers get from cross-generational ties (Harknett and Knab 2007). In 2006, nearly 3.7 million children lived in households composed of parents and grandparents, but research finds that positive parenting is often compromised in such households. Although grandparents may enhance the physical survival of children, they have also been found to have fewer child-centered childrearing practices and harsher discipline strategies (Barnett 2008). Researchers have also found that supportive family networks among low-income black and Latin American women often drain them of resources, can thwart upward mobility, and generate negative social capital and stress (Dominguez and Walkins 2003). Social class polarization, or the loss of stable middle-class families in poor neighborhoods, and the intensification of poverty have left the poor with fewer resources to share. Job loss and welfare cuts have made it more difficult for many families to achieve stability, and geographic mobility and shifting household compositions are common for many living in poverty. The constant and confusing reconfigurations of households can subject children to numerous authority figures; undermine access to privacy, food, and basic necessities; and lead to more physical and sexual abuse of children. Interviewing low-income black men, Alford Young (2004) found that although most of them grew up in single-mother families, they often were unable to describe the composition of the household. What they did recall was a series of problems, crises, and shifts in family structure:

> Crises and uncertainties were common features of family life. Relatives came and went regularly over the years as a response to loss of jobs, the inability to pay rent, or the need to avoid a threatening or problematic resident of their own domicile. . . . The births and departures of siblings throughout their childhood, coupled with temporary (but sometimes lengthy) household hosting of aunts, uncles, and cousins, made family life an unstable, if not altogether turbulent, experience. (Pp. 72–73)

Marriages among those living in poverty are often fragile, but for single mothers, cohabiting and romantic relationships are even more transient. Children living with single mothers who are not cohabiting or involved in romantic relationships with the children's biological fathers often experience numerous changes in family structure, which correlates with high levels of aggressive behavior in children. At least 25 to 30 percent of children born to low-income single mothers who were not living with their male partners experience three or more partnership transitions before age 3 (Osborne and McLanahan 2007). Cohabiting relationships tend to be short-lived; about half of them last a year or less (Avellar and Smock 2005). About 15 to 20 percent of cohabiting women are involved in serial cohabitation, and low-income women have the highest rates of multiple cohabitation (Lichter and Qian 2008). Children in low-income cohabiting families are five times more likely to experience separation than are those in married couple families (Osborne, Manning, and Smock 2007). Cohabiters are less likely than married couples to hold traditional gender or family values and more likely to have jobs that are unstable and to earn lower wages (Blackwell and Lichter 2000). The dissolution of a cohabiting relationship results in an economic decline for both the men and women who were involved, but the consequences are much greater for women. Men experience a 10 percent and women a 33 percent decline in household income when the relationship ends (Avellar and Smock 2005).

Poverty remains prevalent among single-mother households; they are five times more likely than married couple households to be poor (Royce 2009:249). In 2001, the median household income for single-mother African American families was less than $21,000, compared to $29,650 for white single mothers (Conrad and King 2005). Although the difference is not as great for single fathers, they do tend to have lower levels of income and education than married fathers. Poverty is associated with a host of factors that adversely affect children; for example, it is highly associated with low birth weight in infants, the greatest single damaging factor to infant health (Christmas 1996). From infancy onward, children in poor single-mother families have more restricted diets, more health problems and chronic illnesses, and more social and emotional problems (Roosa et al. 2005). Single parents tend to have less education than married parents and live in poorer neighborhoods, both factors that increase the risk to children (Bumpass and McLanahan 1989). Impoverished neighborhoods lack the institutional infrastructure to promote the healthy growth of children (e.g., libraries, parks, recreation centers), and many living in poor areas amid crime, hustling, and shattered families also are completely deprived of middle-class role models. Children living with single mothers, despite race or social class, are more likely than those living with two biological parents to experience school failure, behavioral and psychological problems, delinquency, and illegal drug use (Ellwood and Jencks 2004; Sigle-Rushton and McLanahan 2004).

Poverty and single motherhood can adversely affect the quality of parenting that children experience, beyond authoritarian childrearing practices. Low levels of education, unemployment, poorly paid work, welfare dependency, inadequate housing, hunger, unpaid bills, and living in deteriorated neighborhoods can spill over into harsh and inconsistent parenting practices and even child abuse and neglect. Poor single mothers are often emotionally distressed, and this diminishes their capacity to provide warm, supportive, involved parenting. They spank their children significantly more often than do more affluent mothers, and more frequent spankings contribute to the mental health problems of children and to child abuse (McLoyd 1990; McLeod and Shanahan 1996).

Again, although family violence has been found among people in all social classes, rates of child abuse and neglect are higher in low-income and single-mother families; indeed, poverty is the strongest and most consistent predictor of child abuse. Low-income parents are more likely than other parents to engage in physical discipline, which is the single most common context in which child abuse occurs (Straus and Donnelly 1994). Given stressful living conditions, it is easy to see how physical discipline can turn into physical abuse. In fact, father absence itself is associated with elevated levels of violence against children, with theorists suggesting several factors that might account for this: diminished social control (or less supervision of children), less social capital in neighbors where fathers are absent, the lack of adequate role models, and the stresses of living in poverty (Schwartz 2006). Schwartz sees child abuse as reflecting an elevated care burden in many low-income communities, where the number of children needing care exceeds the availability of both people and resources. Young men in such neighborhoods are especially prone to violence because they spend more time with peers than parents and tend to emulate aggressive forms of masculinity.

Social Policy and the Poor

Poverty is strongly correlated with single motherhood and welfare dependency; thus, the decline in marriage resulted in a dramatic growth in welfare dependency between 1970 and 1990. Many conservative social analysts were as concerned about the separation of marriage and motherhood as they were about the growing welfare budget, and they saw welfare eligibility as a causal factor in promoting nonmarital motherhood (Murray 1984). The U.S. welfare system was born in the 1930s, but from its origins, it was shaped by the fear that welfare benefits would contribute to dependency and undermine the desire of people to work. Thus, the benefits it provides have always been less comprehensive and generous than those provided in other industrialized nations and more likely to be restricted to certain populations defined as needy than broadly available based on citizenship. In addition, the welfare system has also embodied racist and sexist ideologies; for example, it often excluded from benefits those who did domestic and agricultural work, in order to appease Southern whites who feared the loss of cheap African American workers. It also embodied family ideologies that assumed the breadwinner-homemaker family model and sought to provide benefits mostly to widowed women, based on the assumption that they could not do the work of both fathers (earning wages) and mothers (caring for children).

Thus, the migration of African American women from the South and their growing rates of nonmarital childbearing challenged the foundation of the welfare system and, by the 1980s, led to substantial cuts in benefits such as housing and more outcry that single mothers should be employed rather than receive welfare benefits. Political conservatives saw the problem as an erosion of morality and family values among people of color and those living in poor areas, while liberals were more likely to attribute these changes in family structure to the post-industrial economy.

Despite the differences among conservatives and liberals in explaining the growth of the welfare state, images of "welfare queens" and criticism of the "underclass" grew in the popular media, fomenting much controversy. As Gans (1995:6–7) notes, being in the underclass and poor was no longer seen in terms of economics but rather in behavioral terms, with the poverty being linked to sexual promiscuity, laziness, crime, and unwillingness to work. Within this context, Aid to Families With Dependent Children was scrapped in favor of the Personal Responsibility and Work Opportunity Act signed in 1996 by President Clinton, with a promise to "end welfare as we know it." This welfare reform policy placed tighter restrictions on eligibility for welfare receipt; it also imposed a five-year limit on benefits in most states and severed the link between welfare benefits and entitlement to health care benefits through Medicaid. An underlying assumption of welfare reform was that the old system rewarded childbearing, a hypothesis advanced for decades despite much social science research to the contrary. But a strong economy was emerging in the 1990s, and the number of people receiving welfare had already begun to decline. The entry of women into the labor market, however, did not reduce poverty very much because they were confined to low-paying jobs. Moreover, by the early twenty-first century, the booming economy was slowly plummeting, leading to the loss of millions of jobs.

Is Marriage the Answer?

Along with employment, policy analysts suggested that marriage was the solution to the poverty experienced by so many single mothers; in fact, the language embedded in the welfare reform legislation described marriage as "the foundation of a successful society" and "an essential institution that promotes the interests of children" (Jayakody and Cabrera 2002). On the surface, marriage may sound like an ideal solution because most low-income women express a desire to get married, and the preponderance of research evidence finds that there are significant disadvantages for children who grow up in single-parent families. But the marriage solution has generated much controversy and research, most of which suggests the solution is far too simplistic and generally not likely to improve the lives of poor women. For example, many poor women who have the opportunity to marry refuse to do so because they understand the risks—economic, emotional, and physical— of being married to low-income men who lack steady work (Edin 2000). Yet, marriage promotion programs are quite gendered in that they place more pressure on women to marry than men. One study of a marriage education program found that it encouraged poor women to "swallow their rage and grievances against men" and bring their partners into the cultural mainstream of marriage (Huston and Melz 2004).

Even if the economic fortunes of poor women improve, there is scant evidence that marriage yields the same benefits for the poor as it does for more affluent couples. For example, although some argue that married people have higher levels of health, wealth, and well-being than single people and that children benefit from living with two married, biological parents, analysis of national data suggests that for the poor, the benefits to married couples and their children are modest at best (Acs 2007). As noted earlier, studies have found that women in general are less satisfied with their marriages than are men, and unhappy marriages correlate with adverse health outcomes, such as elevated levels of psychological distress and poor health (Hawkins and Booth 2005). Marital unhappiness takes a greater toll on wives than husbands, with unhappy wives having high levels of depression and substance abuse (Coontz 2005).

Marriage, in fact, offers only a marginal and problematic solution to poverty. As O'Connor (2000) notes, scholars must focus more on the political economy that generates jobs for the poor if they hope to offer viable solutions to poverty. Even welfare policies that are premised on the breadwinner-homemaker family ideology and the family wage must be rethought. As Nancy Fraser (1994) argues, promoting gender equity would mean the creation of policies that are antipoverty; that do not leave women open to exploitation and marginalization; and that foster equity in income, respect, and leisure. She proposes several models that might move us beyond policies that are imbued with the logic of men as the primary wage earners, such as a universal breadwinner model that integrates men and women into the labor market in an equitable fashion. A second model might be a caregiver parity model, which supports the caregiving work women or men perform in their families. There are difficulties with both models, but in the end, gender equity in the home and labor market should be the goal.

Conclusion

This chapter has sought to capture the marriage and family experiences of economically marginal couples, specifically those who are in the lower tiers of the working class and those who are poor. Race and gender predict who is most likely to be found in the lower classes, but a class perspective highlights family systems and lifestyles that transcend racial and gender inequalities. Although I have focused on some issues that are more common among such families, such as fragile marriages, single-parent households, and family violence, I have also tried to convey the variety of lifestyles that exist among those in this class. For example, although there is mounting evidence that children who grow up in low-income families experience a host of risk factors and some negative outcomes, most people who grow up poor go on to become responsible, productive adults. Another key point made in this chapter is that although those who are economically marginal are often seen as having a different set of cultural values, those values are typically rooted in social structural forces, such as the economy. Attitudinal surveys typically show that low-income people hold the same set of values as do their more affluent counterparts. Marriage promotion programs, therefore, are based on the faulty premise that the poor do not value marriage as much as others. Finally, social policies aimed at helping the poor have often been based on racist and sexist ideologies and often have done little to alleviate poverty.

6

Families in Global
Economic Context

In this book, I have defined families as essentially care institutions because they originate in efforts to sustain the physical survival of their members. In order to ensure this survival—and thus perpetuate the human species—families across the globe face similar tasks, such as how to distribute family work and economically productive labor; define the roles of men, women, and children; maintain marriage and kin relations; rear children; and effectively manage the family. Rules about families and marriages as social institutions evolved over time within the context of changing economic circumstances, ideologies, and political forces. These rules are typically encoded in laws and policies, so the meaning of the family is socially constructed. While recognizing the intersection of these factors, I have highlighted the saliency of the economy and the place of families within the economy, specifically their social class, in shaping major aspects of family life. Throughout, I have also examined how racial/ethnic and gender inequalities influence the structure and meaning of families, although I maintain that social class position can be seen as an overarching perspective because it often shapes how other social inequalities are enacted. For example, gender is a major social structure that shapes families, but the life experiences and expectations of women in upper-class and lower-class families are quite different. Similarly, racial/ethnic differences between families are typically the result of social disadvantage, which may have resulted in—or fostered the retention or development of—distinct cultural practices. But the cultural practices of low-income families are often quite similar, such as a greater reliance on extended family members, and they tend to wane with economic mobility. This suggests that the cultural behaviors of disadvantaged racial/ethnic groups are often more the result of survival strategies than valued traditions.

Although the chapters on the origin of families and theories of social inequality have broad cross-national applicability, the chapters that focus on social class relate primarily to the United States. As a relatively young nation, it has had a unique history. It lacked a history of feudalism, was freed from the rule of monarchs after independence from England, and had an abundance of resources ripe for development. The ideology of the American Dream championed an open, free, and equal society in which anyone could achieve success and wealth by working hard. This fostered an ethic of individual responsibility that often ignored social structural barriers to success and institutionalized inequalities based on gender, race, and social class. During the twentieth century, the United States became the wealthiest nation in the world, and in the early years following World War II, that wealth led to a decline in economic inequality among people—albeit temporarily (May 1999). For many social theorists, this success was evidence of the virtues of capitalism, technology, innovation, and the acceptance of modern values. Moreover, the sociological study of families was headed by American scholars, and the nation was thought to have the most highly developed, egalitarian family system in the world. However, by the 1970s, not only was social inequality escalating in the United States, but a new global economy was emerging. Thus, another theme throughout this book has been the changing nature of the American social class structure.

Changes in the social class structure were the result primarily of new technologies (such as the computer chip), the rise of the post-industrial (or information and services) economy, and intense efforts among capitalists to garner profits in a rapidly globalizing economy. The rise of a post-industrial economy was predicted amid the prosperity of the 1950s, and by the late 1960s, its impact on the U.S. economy was becoming evident in the gradual demise of industrial jobs. By the twenty-first century, the nation had lost literally millions of industrial jobs, many of which were the very high-paying unionized jobs that had expanded the middle class during the post–World War II era. Economic restructuring began with the loss of blue-collar industrial jobs but eventually expanded to include professional white-collar positions. Contributing to this job loss was the emergence of a global economy, as many nations recovered from the devastation of World War II and began to compete effectively with the United States. The profits of American companies declined during the 1970s, and many sought to recapture their competitive edge by investing heavily in foreign countries, where labor and resources were cheaper (Perrucci and Wysong 2008).

This fostered a global labor market that undermined the wage structure for most American workers, leading to a greater concentration of wealth and of poverty. For example, the big winners in the economic transformation and global market were people with assets worth more than $10 million. The number of people in this category increased 400 percent between 1980 and 2001, and those earning more than $1 million annually received most of the tax breaks (Correspondents 2005). On the other hand, the average worker experienced significant setbacks—the loss of high-paying jobs and benefits, more job insecurity—as the poor faced social policies that curtailed access to welfare, housing, and food. Led by corporate powers that sought to maintain profits by globalizing production and the labor market, the political discourse claimed social welfare policies and organized labor unions were undermining the work ethic of Americans and impeding free markets (Perrucci and Wysong 2008). Still, the rate of unemployment grew and the depth of the economic recession intensified. A 2004 Gallup poll reported that 61 percent of Americans were concerned that they might lose their jobs because of foreign competition (Perrucci and Wysong 2008).

Theorizing Global Inequalities

Although the impact of the global economy was not realized by many until the 1970s, the origins of the global economy and a global perspective of social inequality had begun to emerge in the 1950s. More international travel, involvement of young people in the Peace Corps, and independence movements by nations previously colonized or dominated by Western nations all served to enhance global awareness. A growing critical awareness of the military and economic dominance of the United States and its rising standard of living, the international influence of American universities, and the scholarly development of the concept of core and periphery nations also fostered a global perspective on social inequality (Wallerstein 2004). Core nations were wealthy nations that had dominated in terms of productivity, military power, and wealth, whereas peripheral nations were poor and often had long histories of being colonized by dominant countries. In recent centuries, Western countries had been more responsible for colonizing poor countries, starting with the Netherlands in the 1600s, Britain through the 1800s, and later the United States. Their dominance was based on military prowess, wealth, and the creation of advanced agricultural and then industrial economies, technological development, and mass production. But as discussed in Chapter 1, it was also a result of global exploration; the exploitation of land, labor, and natural resources of poorer nations; and imperialist policies.

Theorists explaining the economic divide between core and peripheral nations in the 1950s drew on the logic of structural functionalism, which saw modernization and industrialization as inevitable and evolutionary forces destined to transform all societies by creating technological innovation and wealth. The question then became why these forces were not working as well in poor countries. This reasoning led to the development of modernization theory, which explained the perpetuation of poverty in poor nations as resulting from psychological characteristics or cultural backwardness of people in poor nations: They simply refused to embrace modern attitudes and ideologies. For example, John Kenneth Galbraith, a noted economist, expounded on the efforts made by the United States to eliminate poverty in India. According to Galbraith, these efforts were meant to thwart the spread of communism but were also motivated by humanitarian concerns over mass starvation. But the farmers in India often refused to embrace modern technologies that would have improved crops or modern values such as reducing the rate of childbearing. Thus, efforts to modernize failed because of resistance to change. More recent work has also linked widespread poverty in India to the legacy of the caste system, the denial of dignity to workers, and the persistent antimodern and antiwoman tendencies of the nation (Glassman et al. 2004).

World systems or dependency theory, on the other hand, proffers an alternative perspective on global patterns of social inequality: It highlights how core countries have exploited periphery countries for literally centuries. The core-periphery concept emerged from the work of Third World scholars, who argued that nations have never been on an equal footing; for example, historically dominant cultures had more value-producing resources such as wealth, land, science, and knowledge (Tilly 2005). One result has been that the economies of poor countries have never been allowed to evolve in a natural fashion, but rather have been controlled and dominated by Western powers. The global dominance of Western powers continues.

These global patterns of social inequality have become entrenched. In 2001, North America had 5 percent of the world's population but was responsible for 30 percent of its industrial production (Tilly 2005). At the other extreme, Africa had 13 percent of the world's population and a mere 2 percent of its industrial production, while Asia (including the rich countries of Japan, South Korea, Taiwan, and Singapore) had a full 61 percent of the world's population and 26 percent of its industrial production. Looked at another way, North America had six times it share of wealth, Asians had less than half their share, and Africans less than one-sixth their share 2005:15). Poverty is defined by the World Bank as living on less than $2 a day, and absolute or extreme poverty as living on less than $1 a day (Stiglitz 2007). Of the more than 6.5 billion people on earth, 40 percent live in poverty—up from 36 percent in 1981. In 2001, nearly one-half (47 percent) of those in Africa lived in extreme poverty (Stiglitz 2007). The lack of economic development in many nations—whether fostered by their own tendency to cling to outmoded technologies and cultural traditions or the exploitative practices of wealthy nations—has resulted in widespread poverty and made it difficult for families to fulfill their core function: the survival of their members.

Race and Ethnicity in Global Perspective

Racial/ethnic tensions have intensified and been transformed by economic decline and global migration patterns, much of it sparked by the pursuit of employment. On the one hand, there have been substantial racial advances in the United States: The nation has elected its first African American president, and surveys report that few people endorse explicitly racist policies, such as job discrimination and segregation. Still, the growing visibility of people of color and the fragile economic position of many white Americans has reignited racial animosities. One study reported than 60 percent of whites felt they had lost ground in the 1990s, and 40 percent believed that fewer jobs for whites was a bigger problem than discrimination against racial minorities (McCall 2001). Young, white working-class males often construct their own identity and sense of maleness by distancing themselves from black people, who they believe are moral, intellectual, and sexual inferiors who are infringing upon the rights of white men (Fine et al. 1997). A study by Lillian Rubin (1994) found that whites tended to lump all racial/ethnic groups into the same category and blame them for compromising the economic and cultural foundations of the country. One result has been the creation of a new entity, "European Americans," intended to organize whites to defend themselves against minorities. As one woman said, "Gee, I'm a 'white person.' I never thought about it at all. But now with the different colored people around, you have to think about it because they're thinking about it all the time" (p. 182).

At the same time, the historic white/black paradigm of race relations has become more blurred by high rates of intermarriage among minorities, more interracial children, more people who claim multiple racial identities, and a growing population of Asian and Latino immigrants. Native Americans and

Asians are most likely to marry interracially, but recent data show that 20 percent of African American men are now marrying outside their race. One in every 40 Americans now identifies as "multiracial," and that figure is expected to rise to one in five by 2050 (Lee and Bean 2004). The internationalization of the work force has led to new patterns of immigration and, in many places, heightened racial and ethnic tensions. The number of illegal immigrants in the United States is estimated at 1 to 5 million, and the 10 million foreign-born Americans in 1970 had spiraled to 30 million by 2000 (Kerbo 2009). In the Americas, the dominant (but not only) flow of immigration is from the south to the north and is attributed to the growing number of political refugees and impoverished people who are willing to risk their lives for a better way of life. One frustrated American explained,

> Everything's changed, and it doesn't make sense. Maybe you get it, but I don't. We can't take care of our people and we keep bringing more and more foreigners in. Look at all the homeless. Why do we need more people here when our own people haven't got a place to sleep? (Rubin 1994:186)

The United States is not alone in experiencing an influx of immigrants: Western Europe is also a popular destination, and the result has been a surge in anti-immigrant and right-wing ideologies (Kerbo 2009). Another shift in immigration patterns has been the number of women who are immigrating to wealthy countries in search of work. Using a racialized gender logic in their hiring practices, some employers have sought "small, foreign females" to work in factories because they are seen as reliable, docile, and willing to work for low wages (Hossfeld 1994). Some recent female immigrants have ended up becoming sex workers, but the majority find work as domestics and nannies for wealthy families, who frequently exploit their vulnerability by providing low wages and exploitative working conditions (Ehrenreich and Hochschild 2003). This has led to a growing number of transnational families with marital partners working and residing in different nations. Although men have a long tradition of leaving their wives and children behind while searching for work in more developed nations, the shift to female immigration has even greater ramifications for families. It separates mothers from children and shifts the wage-earning function to wives, thus undermining the basic foundations of family life.

Families Across the Globe

This book has focused on families being transformed by evolving economic forces, which often spawned new ideologies about the roles of men, women, and children. As discussed earlier, the developmental paradigm saw all families as eventually becoming modernized and taking on the characteristics of Western families; however, while Westernization has been a dominant trend, it has also been contested. In recent decades, many nations have struggled against Western influences in favor of retaining more traditional values, often in protest against what they view as the misguided or even decadent values of the West. This has resulted in a fundamental clash in values that often pits "the West against the rest," as non-Western cultures strive to reclaim their identities, advance their economies, and enhance their political and military standing (Huntington [1993] 2004). In some cases, for example, what Western feminism has rejected as oppressive to women (e.g., genital cutting, the wearing of head coverings) has been redefined by Third World feminists as culturally appropriate. But despite these differences and the diversity of families, there are some major family transitions that have affected people across the globe.

One global trend has been the demise of the male role as wage earner and the entry of women into the labor market. Other than those who are in the privileged class, men are increasingly unable to find employment that pays wages adequate to support their families; in some countries, they can scarcely find work at all. Thus, wives and mothers have been drawn into the labor force—whether by female-typed jobs in the post-industrial economy, or higher-level jobs once reserved for men, or by immigrating to new countries. Women constitute 42 to 45 percent of all workers in the industrialized world; for example, in Japan, the majority of women are in the paid labor force, although they still face discrimination and gender inequity in the home (Sernau 2011). Globally, women—especially mothers—spend more labor hours in work than men. More than half the workers in Asia and Africa are women, and in some places, women are more likely than men to be employed as both agricultural and nonagricultural workers (Kerbo 2009). Latin American women are also increasingly entering the labor market, and trends of male authority and privilege are waning (Sernau 2011:152). Economic development policies in Third World countries now focus heavily on investing in women as workers, which challenges longstanding patriarchal traditions.

The growing presence of women in economically productive work has not led to gender equality, but has exposed the myth of male superiority and upended patriarchal traditions—sometimes to the endangerment of women. For example, Mexican women's work in the *maquiladoras* has been associated with an upsurge in the rape and murder of young women, a pattern of femicide all too often ignored by human rights organizations (Morales and Bejarano 2008). But globalization and feminization of the work force has resulted in greater exposure to and criticism of many gender inequities, such as forcing girls into early marriages and denying women basic human rights. Sexual norms have also changed dramatically in all Western nations; for example, the onset of sexuality precedes marriage, and cohabitation has become the first step in family formation. State-sanctioned marriages are often postponed indefinitely and sometimes foregone (Furstenberg 1999). For some, these patterns portend the demise of families—at least, families ruled by men—but for others, these economic factors portend the empowerment of women and advances in the transition to a more equitable society.

The Persistence of Economic and Social Class Inequality

Laws against discrimination, changing gender norms, migration, and economic necessity have all resulted in notable advances by women and racial/ethnic minorities; however, social class and economic inequalities have increased. Economic inequality is greater in less developed countries, where wealth is concentrated and often held by a few powerful entities and poverty is widespread and the dominant experience of the masses. The concept of social class itself pertains to developed or industrial societies, where there are multiple social classes, including a fairly large middle class. But the transition from an industrial to a post-industrial society, the decline of the middle class, and the merging of social class inequalities with multiple other inequalities have resulted in some scholars questioning the continuing relevance of studying social class. In *The Death of Class,* for example, Pakulski and Waters (1996) argue that social class theory is essentially Marxist and rooted in ideas about industrial production and economic determinism. It was based on the belief in distinct classes, class consciousness, and the transformational capacity of the working class, all of which have become less relevant in advanced capitalist societies. Thus, social classes are dissolving, according to Pakulski and Waters, replaced by the growing importance of state and corporate elites; stratification based on skills and knowledge; and the salience of gender, racial, and ethnic inequalities.

Other scholars, however, believe that although the social class structure in the United States has been transformed, it is important to be able to theorize these changes and place them in global context. Robinson (2004), for example, believes that the global economy exemplifies the Marxist vision of the capitalist economy that ultimately leads to overproduction, squeezing worker salaries and benefits to ensure profit, uprooting poor people and destroying their cultures, and creating global apartheid. What he contends is emerging is a global stratification system in which core and periphery nations will have concentrated pockets of wealth and poverty. But the more important issue, according to Munck (2005), is placing social inequality on national and international political agendas. He suggests that the concept of social exclusion might be used to highlight the fact that many people are being deprived of basic legal, economic, and political rights. But whether one envisions social inequalities in terms of a globalized social class structure or as social exclusion, the fact of their persistence and impact on families remains uncontested.

Bibliography

Acker, Joan. 1990. "Hierarchies, Jobs, Bodies: A Theory of Gendered Organizations." *Gender & Society* 4:139–158.

———. 2006. *Class Questions/Feminist Answers.* Lanham, MD: Rowman & Littlefield.

Acs, Gregory. 2007. "Can We Promote Child Well-Being by Promoting Marriage?" *Journal of Marriage and the Family* 69:1326–1344.

Adams, Bert N. and Suzanne K. Steinmetz. 1993. "Family Theory and Methods in the Classics." Pp. 71–94 in *Sourcebook of Family Theory and Methods: A Contextual Approach,* edited by P. G. Boss, W. J. Doherty, R. LaRossa, W. R. Schumn, and S. K. Steinmetz. New York: Plenum Press.

Allen, Walter R. 1978. "The Search for Applicable Theories of Black Family Life." *Journal of Marriage and the Family* 40:117–129.

———. 1979. "Class, Culture and Family Organization: The Effects of Class and Race of Family Structure in Urban America." *Journal of Contemporary Family Studies* 10:301–313.

———. 2001. "Whatever Tomorrow Brings: African American Families and Government Social Policies." Pp. 125–143 in *One-Third of a Nation: African American Perspectives,* edited by U. J. O. Bailey and L. Morris. Washington, DC: Howard University Press.

Alwin, Duane F. 1984. "Trends in Parental Socialization Values: Detroit, 1958–1983." *American Journal of Sociology* 90:359–382.

Amato, Paul R., Alan Booth, David R. Johnson, and Stacy J. Rogers. 2007. *Alone Together: How Marriage in America is Changing.* Cambridge, MA: Harvard University Press.

Aponte, Robert. 1999. "Ethnic Variation in the Family: The Elusive Trend Toward Convergence." Pp. 111–142 in *Handbook of Marriage and the Family,* edited by M. B. Sussman, S. K. Steinmetz, and G. W. Peterson. New York: Plenum Press.

Asante, M. K. 1987. *The Afrocentric Idea.* Philadelphia: Temple University Press.

Atkinson, Robert D. 2005. "Inequality in the New Knowledge Economy." Pp. 52–68 in *The New Egalitarianism,* edited by A. Giddens and P. Diamond. Malden, MA: Polity Press.

Avellar, Sarah and Pamela J. Smock. 2003. "Has the Price of Motherhood Declined Over Time? A Cross-Cohort Comparison of the Motherhood Wage Penalty." *Journal of Marriage and the Family* 65:597–607.

———. 2005. "The Economic Consequences of the Dissolution of Cohabiting Unions." *Journal of Marriage and the Family* 67:315–328.

Ball, Richard E. and Lynn Robbins. 1986. "Marital Status and Life Satisfaction Among Black Americans." *Journal of Marriage and the Family* 48:389–394.

Baltzell, E. Digby. 1958. *Philadelphia Gentlemen: The Making of a National Upper Class.* Glencoe, IL: Free Press.

Barnett, Melissa A. 2008. "Mother and Grandmother Parenting in Low-Income Three-Generation Rural Households." *Journal of Marriage and the Family* 70 (December):1241–1257.

Bartlett, Donald L. and James B. Steele. 1992. *America: What Went Wrong?* Kansas City, KS: Andrews and McMeel.

Baumrind, Diana. 1966. "Effects of Authoritative Parental Control on Child Behavior." *Child Development* 37:62–86.

Beale, Frances. 1970. "Double Jeopardy: To be Black and Female." Pp. 90–100 in *The Black Woman: An Anthology,* edited by T. Cade. New York: Signet.

Beckert, Sven. 2001. *The Monied Metropolis: New York City and the Consolidation of the American Bourgeoisie, 1850–1896.* New York: Cambridge University Press.

Bernard, Jessie S. [1972] 1982. *The Future of Marriage.* New York: World.

Billingsley, Andrew. 1968. *Black Families in White America.* Englewood Cliffs, NJ: Prentice-Hall.

Blackwell, Debra L. and Daniel T. Lichter. 2000. "Mate Selection Among Married and Cohabiting Couples." *Journal of Family Issues* 21:275–302.

Blau, Peter M. and Otis Dudley Duncan. 1967. *The American Occupational Structure.* New York: John Wiley & Sons.

Blee, K. M. and A. R. Tickamyer. 1995. "Racial Differences in Men's Attitudes About Women's Gender Roles." *Journal of Marriage and the Family* 57:21–30.

Blum, Linda M. and Theresa Deussen. 1996. "Negotiating Independent Motherhood: Working-Class African American Women Talk About Marriage and Motherhood." *Gender & Society* 10:199–211.

Blumberg, Paul M. and P. W. Paul. 1975. "Continuities and Discontinuities in Upper-Class Marriages." *Journal of Marriage and the Family* 37:63–77.

Blumer, Herbert. 1969. *Symbolic Interactionism: Perspective and Method.* Englewood Cliffs, NJ: Prentice-Hall.

Bobo, Lawrence. 2000. "Race and Beliefs About Affirmative Action: Assessing the Effects of Interests, Group Threat, Ideology, and Racism." Pp. 137–164 in *Racialized Politics: The Debate About Racism in America,* edited by D. O. Sears, J. Sidanius, and L. Bobo. Chicago and London: University of Chicago Press.

Bogger, Tommy L. 1997. *Free Blacks in Norfolk, Virginia 1790–1860: The Darker Side of Freedom.* Charlottesville: University Press of Virginia.

Bonilla-Silva, Eduardo. 2006. *Racism Without Racists: Color-Blind Racism and the Persistence of Racial Inequality in the United States.* Lanham, MD: Rowman & Littlefield.

Bound, John and Laura Dresser. 1999. "Losing Ground: The Erosion of the Relative Earnings of African American Women During the 1980s." Pp. 61–104 in *Latinas and African American Women at Work: Race, Gender, and Economic Inequality,* edited by I. Brown. New York: Russell Sage Foundation.

Bowser, Benjamin P. 2007. *Black Middle Class: Social Mobility—and Vulnerability.* Boulder, CO: Lynne Rienner.

Breines, Wini and Linda Gordon. 1983. "The New Scholarship on Family Violence." *Signs: Journal of Women in Culture and Society* 8:490–531.

Brewer, Rose. 1993. "Theorizing Race, Class, and Gender: The New Scholarship of Black Feminist Intellectuals and Black Women's Labor." Pp. 13–30 in *Theorizing Black Feminisms: The Visionary Pragmatism of Black Women,* edited by S. M. James and A. P. A. Busia. London and New York: Routledge.

Brooks, David. 2000. *Bobos in Paradise: The New Upper Class and How They Got There.* New York: Simon & Schuster.

———. 2003. "Bobos in Paradise: The New Upper Class and How They Got There." Pp. 161–172 in *Wealth and Poverty in America: A Reader,* edited by D. Conley. Malden, MA: Blackwell.

Browne, Irene. 2000. "Opportunities Lost? Race, Industrial Restructuring, and Employment Among Young Women Heading Households." *Social Forces* 78:907–929.

Buchmann, Claudia and Thomas A. DiPrete. 2006. "The Growing Female Advantage in College Completion: The Role of Family Background and Academic Achievement." *American Sociological Review* 71:515–541.

Buechler, Steven M. 2008. *Critical Sociology.* Boulder, CO: Paradigm.

Bulanda, Jennifer Roebuck and Susan L. Brown. 2007. "Race-Ethnic Differences in Marital Quality and Divorce." *Social Science Research* 36:945–967.

Bumpass, Larry and Sara McLanahan. 1989. "Unmarried Motherhood: Recent Trends, Composition, and Black-White Differences." *Demography* 26:279–287.

Burgess, E. W. and H. J. Locke. 1953. *The Family: From Institution to Companionship.* New York: American Book.

Burr, Wesley R., Geoffrey K. Leigh, Randall D. Day, and John Constantine. 1979. "Symbolic Interactionism and the Family." Pp. 42–111 in *Contemporary Theories About the Family,* vol. 2, edited by W. R. Burr, R. Hill, F. I. Nye, and I. L. Reiss. New York: Free Press.

Burton, Linda M., Eduardo Bonilla-Silva, Victor Ray, Rose Buckelew, and Elizabeth Hordge Freeman. 2010. "Critical Race Theories, Colorism, and the Decade's Research on Families of Color." *Journal of Marriage and the Family* 72:440–459.

Calhoun, Cheshire. 1997. "Family Outlaws: Rethinking the Connection Between Feminism, Lesbianism, and the Family." Pp. 131–150 in *Feminism and Families,* edited by H. L. Nelson. New York: Routledge.

Camhi, Jane Jerome. 2007. "Women Against Women: American Antisuffragism, 1880–1920." Pp. 225–239 in *Understanding Inequality: The Intersection of Race/Ethnicity, Class, and Gender,* edited by B. A. Arrighi. Lanham, MD: Rowman & Littlefield.

Cancio, A. Silvia, T. David Evans, and David J. Maume, Jr. 1996. "Reconsidering the Declining Significance of Race: Racial Differences in Early Career Wages." *American Sociological Review* 61:541–556.

Carnegie, Andrew. 1900. *The Gospel of Wealth and Other Timely Essays.* New York: Century.

Chafetz, J. S. 1999. *Handbook of the Sociology of Gender.* New York: Kluwer Academic/Plenum.

Cherlin, Andrew J. 1992. *Marriage, Divorce, Remarriage (Revised and Enlarged Edition).* Cambridge, MA: Harvard University Press.

Cherlin, Andrew. 2004. "The Deinstitutionalization of Marriage." *Journal of Marriage and the Family* 66:848–861.

———. 2008. *Public and Private Families: An Introduction.* New York: McGraw-Hill.

———. 2009. *Marriage-Go-Round: The State of Marriage and the Family in America Today.* New York: Alfred A. Knopf.

———. 2010a. "Demographic Trends in the United States: A Review of Research in the 2000s." *Journal of Marriage and the Family* 72:403–419.

———. 2010b. *Public and Private Families: An Introduction.* New York: McGraw-Hill.

Cherlin, Andrew, Caitlin Cross-Barnet, Linda M. Burton, and Raymond Garrett-Peters. 2008. "Promises They Can Keep: Low-Income Women's Attitudes Towards Motherhood, Marriage, and Divorce." *Journal of Marriage and the Family* 70:919–933.

Christmas, J. J. 1996. "The Health of African Americans." Pp. 95–126 in *The State of Black America 1966,* edited by A. Rowe and J. M. Jeffries. New York: National Urban League.

Clark, Kenneth B. 1965. *Dark Ghetto: Dilemmas of Social Power.* New York: Harper & Row.

Coleman, James. 1988. "Social Capital in the Creation of Human Capital." *American Journal of Sociology* 94:S95–S120.

Collins, Patricia Hill. 1990. *Black Feminist Thought: Knowledge, Consciousness, and the Politics of Empowerment.* Boston: Unwin Hyman.

———. 1994. "Shifting the Center: Race, Class, and Feminist Theorizing About Motherhood." Pp. 45–66 in *Mothering: Ideology, Experience, and Agency,* edited by E. N. Glenn, G. Chang, and L. R. Forcey. New York: Routledge.

———. 2004. *Black Sexual Politics: African Americans, Gender, and the New Racism.* New York and London: Routledge.

Collins, R. 1986. *Weberian Sociological Theory.* New York: Cambridge University Press.

Collins, Randall. 1975. *Conflict Sociology: Toward an Explanatory Science.* New York: Academic Press.

Coltrane, Scott and Michelle Adams. 2008. *Gender and Families.* Lanham, MD: Rowman & Littlefield.

Conley, Dalton. 1999. *Being Black, Living in the Red: Race, Wealth, and Social Policy in America.* Berkeley: University of California Press.

Connelly, Cynthia D., Rae R. Newton, John Landsverk, and Gregory A. Aarons. 2000. "Assessment of Intimate Partner Violence Among High-Risk Postpartum Mothers." *Women & Health* 31:21–37.

Conrad, Cecilia A. and Marcy C. King. 2005. "Single-Mother Families in the Black Community: Economic Context and Policies." Pp. 163–174 in *African Americans in the U. S. Economy,* edited by C. A. Conrad, J. Whitehead, P. Mason, and J. Stewart. Lanham, MD: Rowman & Littlefield.

Cookson, Peter W. and Caroline Hodges Persell. 1985. *Preparing for Power: America's Elite Boarding Schools.* New York: Basic Books.

Coontz, Stephanie. 1992. *The Way We Never Were: American Families and the Nostalgia Trap.* New York: Basic Books.

———. 2005. *Marriage, a History: From Obedience to Intimacy, or How Love Conquered Marriage.* New York: Viking Penguin.

———. 2007. "Historical Perspectives on Family Diversity." Pp. 63–80 in *Shifting the Center: Understanding Contemporary Families,* edited by S. J. Ferguson. New York: McGraw-Hill.

Correspondents of The New York Times. (2005). *Class Matters.* New York: Times Books.

Coser, Rose Laub. [1964] 2004. "The Family: Its Structure and Functions." Pp. 13–21 in *Families and Society: Classic and Contemporary Readings,* edited by S. Coltrane. Belmont, CA: Wadsworth/Thomson Learning.

Cott, Nancy F. 2000. *Public Vows: A History of Marriage and the Nation.* Boston: Harvard University Press.

Crenshaw, Kimberle Williams. 1997. "Beyond Racism and Misogyny: Black Feminism and 2 Live Crew." Pp. 549–568 in *Women Transforming Politics: An Alternative Reader,* edited by C. J. Cohen, K. B. Jones, and J. C. Tronto. New York and London: New York University Press.

Cromwell, Adelaide M. 1994. *The Other Brahmins: Boston's Black Upper Class, 1750–1950.* Fayetteville: University of Arkansas Press.

Dabel, Jane E. 2002. "African American Women and Household Composition in New York City, 1827–1877." Pp. 60–72 in *Black Cultures and Race Relations,* edited by J. L. Conyers, Jr. Chicago: Burnham.

"Dancing in the Downturn." 2009, January 15. *The Economist* (http://www.economist.com/node/12936559).

Davis, A. and R. J. Havighurst. 1946. "Social Class and Color Differences in Child-Rearing." *American Sociological Review* 2:698–710.

Davis, Kingsley and Wilbert E. Moore. 1944. "Some Principles of Stratification." *American Sociological Review* 10:242–249.

Dickerson, Bette J. 1995. *African American Single Mothers: Understanding Their Lives and Families.* Thousand Oaks, CA: Sage.

Dickerson, Debra J. 2000. *An American Story.* New York: Anchor Books.

Dill, Bonnie Thornton. 1979. "The Dialectic of Black Womanhood." *Signs: Journal of Women in Culture and Society* 4:543–555.

———. 1988. "Our Mothers' Grief: Racial Ethnic Women and the Maintenance of Families." *Journal of Family History* 13:415–431.

Domhoff, G. William. 2006. *Who Rules America?* New York: McGraw-Hill.

Dominguez, Silvia and Celeste Walkins. 2003. "Creating Networks for Survival and Mobility: Social Capital Among African-American and Latin-American Low-Income Mothers." *Social Problems* 50:111–135.

Duiker, W. T. and J. Spielvogel. 1994. *World History VII Since 1500.* St. Paul, MN: West.

Dunaway, Wilma A. 2003. *The African-American Family in Slavery and Emancipation.* New York: Cambridge University Press.

Dye, Thomas R. 1995. *Who's Running America? The Clinton Years.* Upper Saddle River, NJ: Prentice Hall.

Edin, Kathryn. 2000. "What Do Low-Income Single Mothers Say About Marriage?" *Social Problems* 47:112–133.

Edin, Kathryn and Maria Kefalas. 2005. "Unmarried With Children." *Contexts* 4:16–22.

Edin, Kathryn and Rebecca Joyce Kissane. 2010. "Poverty and the American Family: A Decade in Review." *Journal of Marriage and the Family* 72:460–479.

Ehrenreich, Barbara and Arlie Russell Hochschild. 2003. *Global Woman: Nannies, Maids, and Sex Workers in the New Economy.* New York: Metropolitan Books.

Ellwood, David T. and Christopher Jencks. 2004. "The Spread of Single-Parent Families in the United States Since 1960." Pp. 25–65 in *Future of the Family,* edited by D. P. Moynihan, T. M. Smeeding, and L. Rainwater. New York: Russell Sage Foundation.

Elmelech, Yuval. 2008. *Transmitting Inequality: Wealth and the American Family.* Lanham, MD: Rowman & Littlefield.

England, Paula. 2010. "The Gender Revolution: Uneven and Stalled." *Gender & Society* 24:149–166.

Esping-Anderson, Gosta. 2007. "Equal Opportunities and the Welfare State." *Contexts* 6:23–27.

Farrell, Betty G. 1993. *Elite Families: Class and Power in Nineteenth-Century Boston.* Albany: State University of New York Press.

Farrington, Keith and Ely Chertok. 1993. "Social Conflict Theories of the Family." Pp. 357–381 in *Sourcebook of Family Theories and Methods: A Contextual Approach,* edited by P. G. Boss, W. J. Doherty, R. LaRossa, W. R. Schumn, and S. K. Steinmetz. New York: Plenum Press.

Ferree, Myra Marx. 2010. "Filling the Glass: Gender Perspectives on Families." *Journal of Marriage and the Family* 72:420–439.

Ferree, Myra Marx and Beth B. Hess. 1994. *Controversy and Coalition: The New Feminist Movement Across Three Decades of Change*. New York: Twayne.

Fine, M., L. Weis, J. Addleston, and J. Marusza. 1997. "(In)secure Times: Constructing White Working-Class Masculinities in the Late 20th Century." *Gender & Society* 11:52–68.

Firestone, Shulamith. 1970. *The Dialectic of Sex: The Case for Feminist Revolution*. New York: William Morrow.

Frank, Robert. 2007. *Richistan: A Journey Through the American Wealth Boom and the Lives of the New Rich*. New York: Crown.

Franklin, Donna L. 1997. *Ensuring Inequality: The Structural Transformation of the African-American Family*. New York: Oxford University Press.

———. 2000. *What's Love Got to Do With It? Understanding and Healing the Rift Between Black Men and Women*. New York: Touchstone.

Fraser, Nancy. 1994. "After the Family Wage: Gender Equity and the Welfare State." *Political Theory* 22:591–618.

Frazier, E. Franklin. 1948. *The Negro Family in the United States*. New York: Dryden Press.

———. [1939] 1957. *The Negro in the United States*. New York: Macmillan.

Friedan, Betty. 1963. *The Feminine Mystique*. New York: Norton.

Fuchs, Lawrence H. 1990. *The American Kaleidoscope: Race, Ethnicity, and the Civic Culture*. Middletown, CT: Wesleyan University Press.

Furdyna, Holly E., M. Belinda Tucker, and Angela D. James. 2008. "Relative Spousal Earnings and Marital Happiness Among African American and White Women." *Journal of Marriage and the Family* 70:332–344.

Furstenberg, F. F. 1966. "Industrialization and the American Family: A Look Backward." *American Sociological Review* 31:326–337.

Furstenberg, F. 1999. "Is the Modern Family a Threat to Children's Health?" *Society* 36(July/August): 30–37.

Furstenberg, F. F. 2007. "The Making of the Black Family: Race and Class in Qualitative Studies in the Twentieth Century." *Annual Review of Sociology* 33:429–448.

Gans, Herbert J. 1995. *The War Against the Poor: The Underclass and Antipoverty Policy*. New York: Basic Books.

Gibson-Davis, Christina M. 2008. "Family Structure Effects on Maternal and Paternal Parenting in Low-Income Families." *Journal of Marriage and the Family* 70:452–465.

Giddens, Anthony. 1992. *The Transformation of Intimacy: Sexuality, Love and Eroticism in Modern Societies*. Stanford, CA: Stanford University Press.

Gilbert, Dennis. 2003. *The American Class Structure: In an Age of Growing Inequality*. Belmont, CA: Thomson Wadsworth.

———. 2008. *The American Class Structure in an Age of Growing Inequality*. Thousand Oaks, CA: Sage.

Gittins, Diana. 1993. *The Family in Question: Changing Households and Familiar Ideologies*. Basingstoke, UK: Macmillan.

Glassman, Ronald M., William H. Swatos, Jr., and Barbara J. Denison. 2004. *Social Problems in Global Perspective*. Lanham, MD: University Press of America.

Glenn, Evelyn Nakano. 1983. "Split Households, Small Producer, and the Dual Wage Earner: An Analysis of Chinese American Family Strengths." *Journal of Marriage and the Family* 45:35–46.

Goldthorpe, J. E. 1987. *Family Life in Western Societies: A Historical Sociology of Family Relationships in Britain and North America*. Cambridge: Cambridge University Press.

Goodsell, Willystine. 1934. *A History of Marriage and the Family*. New York: Macmillan.

Goodwin, Paula Y. 2003. "African American and European American Women's Marital Well-Being." *Journal of Marriage and the Family* 65:550–560.

Gordon, Linda. 1976. *Woman's Body, Woman's Right: A Social History of Birth Control in America*. New York: Grossman.

Graham, Katharine. 1997. *Personal History*. New York: Vintage Books.

Graham, Lawrence Otis. 1999. *Our Kind of People: Inside America's Black Upper Class*. New York: HarperCollins.

Greene, Felix. 1971. *The Enemy*. London: Random House.

Grusky, David B. and Szonia Szelenyi. 2006. *Inequality: Classic Readings in Race, Class, and Gender*. Boulder, CO: Westview.

Gutman, Herbert G. 1976. *The Black Family in Slavery and Freedom, 1750–1925*. New York: Pantheon.

Hackstaff, Karla B. 2004. "Wives' Marital Work in a Culture of Divorce." Pp. 135–146 in *Families and Society*, edited by S. Coltrane. Belmont, CA: Wadsworth/Thomson.

Hale, Janice E. 1986. *Black Children: Their Roots, Cultures, and Learning Styles*. Baltimore: Johns Hopkins University Press.

Hall, Peter Dobken. 1992. "The Empty Tomb: The Making of a Dynastic Identity." Pp. 255–348 in *Lives in Trust: The Fortunes of Dynastic Families in Late Twentieth-Century America*, edited by G. E. Marcus. Boulder, CO: Westview.

Hareven, Tamara K. 1991. "The History of the Family and the Complexity of Social Change." *American Historical Review* 96:95–124.

Harknett, Kristen and Jean Knab. 2007. "More Kin, Less Support: Multipartnered Fertility and Perceived Support Among Mothers." *Journal of Marriage and the Family* 69:237–253.

Harknett, Kristen and Sara S. McLanahan. 2004. "Racial and Ethnic Differences in Marriage After the Birth of a Child." *American Sociological Review* 69:790–811.

Harrington, Michael. 1962. *The Other America: Poverty in the United States*. Baltimore: Penguin.

Hartmann, Heidi. [1977] 2005. "Capitalism, Patriarchy, and Job Segregation by Sex." Pp. 53–57 in *Great Divides: Readings in Social Inequality in the United States*, edited by T. M. Shapiro. Boston: McGraw-Hill.

Harvey, David. 2005. *A Brief History of Neoliberalism*. New York: Oxford University Press.

Hawkins, Daniel and Alan Booth. 2005. "Unhappily Ever After: Effects of Long-Term, Low-Quality Marriages on Well-Being." *Social Forces* 84:451–471.

Herbert, Bob. 2004. "Jobless and Ignored." *Kansas City Star*, B5.

Herrnstein, Richard J. and Charles Murray. 1994. *The Bell Curve: Intelligence and the Class Structure in American Life.* New York: Free Press.

Hertz, Rosanna. 2006. *Single by Chance, Mothers by Choice: How Women are Choosing Parenthood Without Marriage and Changing the American Family.* New York: Oxford.

Hill, E. Jeffrey. 2005. "Work-Family Facilitation and Conflict, Working Fathers and Mothers, Work-Family Stressors and Support." *Journal of Family Issues* 26: 793–819.

Hill, Nancy E., Velma McBride Murry, and Valerie D. Anderson. 2005. "Sociocultural Contexts of African American Families." Pp. 21–44 in *African American Family Life: Ecological and Cultural Diversity,* edited by V. C. McLoyd, N. E. Hill, and K. A. Dodge. New York: Guilford Press.

Hill, Robert B. 1972. *The Strengths of Black Families.* New York: Emerson Hall.

———. 2001. "Race, Class, and Culture: Common Pitfalls in Research on African American Families." Pp. 99–123 in *One-Third of a Nation: African American Perspectives,* edited by U. J. O. Bailey and L. Morris. Washington, DC: Howard University Press.

Hill, Shirley A. 1999. *African American Children: Socialization and Development in Families.* Thousand Oaks, CA: Sage.

———. 2005. *Black Intimacies: A Gender Perspective on Families and Relationships.* Walnut Creek, CA: AltaMira Press.

Hill, Shirley A. and Mary K. Zimmerman. 1995. "Valiant Girls and Vulnerable Boys: The Impact of Gender and Race on Mothers' Caregiving for Chronically Ill Children." *Journal of Marriage and the Family* 57:43–53.

Hine, Darlene Clark and Kathleen Thompson. 1998. *A Shining Thread of Hope.* New York: Broadway Books.

Hochschild, Arlie Russell. 1983. *The Managed Heart: Commercialization of Human Feeling.* Berkeley and Los Angeles: University of California Press.

———. 1989. *The Second Shift: Working Parents and the Revolution at Home.* New York: Viking.

Hook, Jennifer L. and Satvika Chalasani. 2008. "Gendered Expectations? Reconsidering Single Fathers' Child-Care Time." *Journal of Marriage and the Family* 70:978–990.

Hossfeld, K. J. 1994. "Hiring Immigrant Women: Silcon Valley's 'Simple Formula.'" Pp. 65–93 in *Women of Color in U.S. Society,* edited by M. B. Zinn and B. T. Dill. Philadelphia: Temple University Press.

Hout, Michael. 2008. "How Class Works: Objective and Subjective Aspects of Class Since the 1970s." Pp. 25–64 in *Social Class: How Does it Work?* edited by A. Lareau and D. Conley. New York: Russell Sage Foundation.

Huntington, Samuel P. [1993] 2004. "The Clash of Civilizations." Pp. 36–43 in *The Globalization Reader,* edited by F. J. Lechner and J. Boli. Oxford: Blackwell.

Hurst, Charles E. 2004. *Social Inequality: Forms, Causes, and Consequences*. Boston: Pearson Education.

Huston, Ted L. and Heidi Melz. 2004. "The Case for (Promoting) Marriage: The Devil Is in the Details." *Journal of Marriage and the Family* 66:943–958.

Ingoldsby, Bron B. 2006. "The History of the Euro-Western Family." Pp. 41–59 in *Families in Global and Multicultural Perspective*, edited by B. B. Ingoldsby and S. D. Smith. Thousand Oaks, CA: Sage.

Ingoldsby, Bron B., Suzanne R. Smith, and J. Elizabeth Miller. 2004. *Exploring Family Theories*. Los Angeles: Roxbury.

Irwin, George. 2008. *Super Rich: The Rise of Inequality in Britain and the United States*. Malden, MA: Polity.

Jacobs, Jerry and Kathleen Gerson. 2004. *The Time Divide: Work, Family, and Gender Inequality*. Cambridge, MA: Harvard University Press.

Jarrett, Robin L. 1994. "Living Poor: Family Life Among Single Parent, African-American Women." *Social Problems* 41:30–50.

Jayakody, Rukmalie and Natasha Cabrera. 2002. "What Are the Choices for Low-Income Families? Cohabitation, Marriage, and Remaining Single." Pp. 85–95 in *Just Living Together: Implications of Cohabitation on Families, Children, and Social Policy*, edited by A. Booth and A. C. Crounter. Mahwah, NJ: L. Erlbaum Associates.

Jayakody, Rukmalie, Arland Thornton, and William G. Axinn. 2008. *International Family Change: Ideational Perspectives*. New York: Lawrence Erlbaum.

John, Daphne and Beth Anne Shelton. 1997. "The Production of Gender Among Black and White Women and Men: The Case of Household Labor." *Sex Roles* 36:171–193.

Johnson, Michael P. 1995. "Patriarchal Terrorism and Common Couple Violence: Two Forms of Violence Against Women." *Journal of Marriage and the Family* 57:283–294.

Jones, Jacqueline. 1985. *Labor of Love, Labor of Sorrow: Black Women, Work, and the Family from Slavery to the Present*. New York: Basic Books.

Kanter, Rosabeth Moss. 1977. *Work and Family in the United States: A Critical Review and Agenda for Research and Policy*. New York: Russell Sage Foundation.

Kendall, Diana Elizabeth. 2002. *The Power of Good Deeds: Privileged Women and the Social Reproduction of the Upper Class*. Lanham, MD: Roman & Littlefield.

Kennedy, S. and L. Bumpass. 2008. "Cohabitation and Children's Living Arrangements." *Demographic Research* 19:1663–1692.

Kerbo, Harold R. 2009. *Social Stratification and Inequality: Class Conflict in Historical, Comparative, and Global Perspective*. New York: McGraw-Hill.

Kingsbury, Nancy and John Scanzoni. 1993. "Structural-functionalism." Pp. 195–217 in *Sourcebook of Family Theories and Methods: A Contextual Approach*, edited by P. G. Boss, W. J. Doherty, R. LaRossa, W. R. Schumn, and S. K. Steinmetz. New York: Plenum Press.

Kivisto, Peter. 2002. *Multiculturalism in a Global Society*. Oxford, UK and Malden, MA: Blackwell.

Kline, Wendy. 2001. *Building a Better Race: Gender, Sexuality, and Eugenics from the Turn of the Century to the Baby Boom.* Berkeley and Los Angeles: University of California Press.

Knoester, Chris, Richard J. Petts, and David J. Eggebeen. 2007. "Commitments to Fathering and the Well-Being and Social Participation of New, Disadvantaged Fathers." *Journal of Marriage and the Family* 69:991–1004.

Kohn, Melvin L. 1963. "Social-Class and Parent-Child Relationships." *American Journal of Sociology* 63:471–480.

Komarovsky, Mirra. 1962. *Blue-Collar Marriage.* New York: Vintage Books.

Koos, Earl Lomon. 1946. *Families in Trouble.* New York: King's Crown Press.

Lacy, Karyn R. 2007. *Blue-Chip Black: Race, Class, and Status in the New Black Middle Class.* Berkeley and Los Angeles: University of California Press.

Lamanna, Mary Ann. 2002. *Emile Durkheim on the Family.* Thousand Oaks, CA: Sage.

Landry, Bart. 1987. *The New Black Middle Class.* Berkeley: University of California Press.

———. 2000. *Black Working Wives: Pioneers of the American Family Revolution.* Berkeley: University of California Press.

Lansford, J. E., K. Deater-Deckard, K. A. Dodge, J. E. Bates, and G. S. Petit. 2004. "Ethnic Differences in the Link Between Physical Discipline and Later Adolescent Externalizing Behaviors." *Journal of Child Psychology and Psychiatry* 45:801–812.

Lareau, Annette. 2002. "Invisible Inequality: Social Class and Childrearing in Black Families and White Families." *American Sociological Review* 67:747–776.

———. 2003. *Unequal Childhoods: Class, Race, and Family Life.* Berkeley: University of California Press.

LaRossa, Ralph and Donald C. Reitzes. 1993. "Symbolic Interactionism and Family Studies." Pp. 135–163 in *Sourcebook of Family Theories and Methods: A Contextual Approach,* edited by P. G. Boss, W. J. Doherty, R. LaRossa, W. R. Schumn, and S. K. Steinmetz. New York: Plenum Press.

Lasch, Christopher. 1977. *Haven in a Heartless World: The Family Besieged.* New York: Basic Books.

Laslett, Barbara and Barrie Thorne. 1997. "Life Histories of a Movement: An Introduction." Pp. 1–27 in *Feminist Sociology: Life Histories of a Movement,* edited by B. Laslett and B. Thorne. New Brunswick, NJ: Rutgers University Press.

Lawson, Erma Jean and Aaron Thompson. 1999. *Black Men and Divorce.* Thousand Oaks, CA: Sage.

Lee, Jennifer and Frank D. Bean. 2004. "America's Changing Color Line: Immigration, Race/Ethnicity, and Multiracial Identification." *Annual Review of Sociology* 30:221–242.

Leeder, Elaine. 2004. *Family in Global Perspective: A Gendered Journey.* Thousand Oaks, CA: Sage.

Lehmann, Jennifer M. 1995. "The Question of Caste in Modern Society: Durkheim's Contradictory Theories of Race, Class, and Sex." *American Sociological Review* 60:566–585.

LeMasters, E. E. 1975. *Blue-Collar Aristocrats: Lifestyles at a Working-Class Tavern.* Madison: University of Wisconsin.

Levine, Steven B. 1980. "The Rise of the American Boarding Schools and the Development of a National Upper Class." *Social Problems* 28:63–94.

Lewis, D. K. 1975. "The Black Family: Socialization and Sex Roles." *Phylon* 36:221–238.

Lichter, Daniel T. and Zhenchao Qian. 2008. "Serial Cohabitation and the Marital Life Course." *Journal of Marriage and the Family* 70:861–878.

Lomnitz, Larissa Adler de and Marisol Pérez Lizaur. 1987. *A Mexican Elite Family, 1820–1980: Kinship, Class, and Culture.* Princeton, NJ: Princeton University Press.

Lorber, Judith. 1998. *Gender Inequality: Feminist Theories and Politics.* Los Angeles: Roxbury.

Lytton, Hugh and David M. Romney. 1991. "Parents' Differential Socialization of Boys and Girls: A Meta-Analysis." *Psychological Bulletin* 109:267–296.

Marger, Martin N. 2008. *Social Inequality: Patterns and Processes.* New York: McGraw-Hill.

May, Elaine Tyler. 1999. *Homeward Bound: American Families in the Cold War Era.* New York: Basic Books.

Mayer, Kurt B. and Walter Buckley. 1970. *Class and Society.* New York: Random House.

McAdoo, H. P. 1998. "African-American Families: Strengths and Realities." Pp. 17–30 in *Resiliency in African American Families,* edited by H. I. McCubbin, E. A. Thompson, A. I. Thompson, and J. A. Futrell. Thousand Oaks, CA: Sage.

McCall, Leslie. 2001. *Complex Inequality: Gender, Class, and Race in the New Economy.* New York: Routledge.

McLanahan, S., I. Garfinkel, N. Reichman, J. Teitler, M. J. Carlson, and C. N. Audigier. 2003. *The Fragile Families and Child Wellbeing Study: Baseline National Report.* Princeton, NJ: Princeton University Press.

McLeod, J. D. and M. J. Shanahan. 1996. "Trajectories of Poverty and Children's Mental Health." *Journal of Health and Social Behavior* 37:207–220.

McLoyd, V. C. 1990. "The Impact of Economic Hardships on Black Families and Children: Psychological Distress, Parenting, and Socioemotional Development." *Child Development* 61:311–346.

Meier, August and David Lewis. 1959. "History of the Negro Upper Class in Atlanta, Georgia, 1890–1958." *Journal of Negro Education* 28:128–139.

Mills, C. Wright. 1956. *The Power Elite.* New York: Oxford University Press.

Mintz, S. and S. Kellogg. 1988. *Domestic Revolutions: A Social History of American Family Life.* Cambridge, MA: Belknap Press of Harvard University Press.

Morales, M. Cristina and Cynthia Bejarano. 2008. "Border Sexual Conquest: A Framework for Gendered and Racial Sexual Violence." Pp. 181–198 in *Globalization and America: Race, Human Rights, and Inequality,* edited by A. J. Hattery, D. G. Embrick, and E. Smith. Lanham, MD: Rowman & Littlefield.

Moynihan, Daniel Patrick. 1965. *The Negro Family: The Case for National Action.* Washington, DC: Office of Policy Planning and Research.

Munck, Ronaldo. 2005. "Social Exclusion: New Inequality Paradigm for the Era of Globalization?" Pp. 31–59 in *The Blackwell Companion to Social Inequalities*, edited by M. Romero and E. Margolis. Malden, MA: Blackwell.

Murray, C. 1984. *Losing Ground: American Social Policy 1950–1980*. New York: Basic Books.

Myrdal, Gunnar. 1944. *An American Dilemma: The Negro Problem and Modern Democracy*. New York: Harper & Brothers.

Newsome, Yvonne D. and F. Nii-Amoo DoDoo. 2006. "Reversal of Fortune: Explaining the Decline in Black Women's Earnings." Pp. 159–183 in *Race, Work, and the Family in the Lives of African Americans*, edited by M. Durr and S. A. Hill. Lanham, MD: Rowman & Littlefield.

Nobles, Wade W. 1974. "Africanity: Its Role in Black Families." *Black Scholar* 5:10–17.

Noel, Donald. 1968. "A Theory of the Origin of Ethnic Stratification." *Social Problems* 16:157–172.

O'Connor, Alice. 2000. "Poverty Research and Policy for the Post-Welfare Era." *Annual Review of Sociology* 26:547–562.

O'Connor, Thomas H. 2006. *The Athens of America: Boston, 1825–1845*. Amherst: University of Massachusetts Press.

Ogbu, John U. 1981. "Origins of Human Competence: A Cultural-Ecological Perspective." *Child Development* 52:413–429.

Osborne, Cynthia, Wendy D. Manning, and Pamela J. Smock. 2007. "Marriage and Cohabiting Parents' Relationship Stability: A Focus on Race and Ethnicity." *Journal of Marriage and the Family* 69:1345–1366.

Osborne, Cynthia and Sara McLanahan. 2007. "Partnership Instability and Child Well-Being." *Journal of Marriage and the Family* 69:1065–1083.

Osmond, Marie and Barrie Thorne. 1993. "Feminist Theories: The Social Construction of Gender in Families and Society." Pp. 591–622 in *Sourcebook on Family Theories and Methods: A Contextual Approach*, edited by P. Boss, W. J. Doherty, R. LaRossa, W. R. Schumn, and S. K. Steinmetz. New York: Plenum.

Ostrander, Susan A. 1984. *Women of the Upper Class*. Philadelphia: Temple University Press.

Page, Benjamin I. and Lawrence R. Jacobs. 2009. *Class War? What Americans Really Think About Economic Inequality*. Chicago: University of Chicago Press.

Pakulski, Jan and Malcolm Waters. 1996. *The Death of Class*. Thousand Oaks, CA: Sage.

Parsons, T. and R. Bales. 1955. *Family Socialization and Interaction Processes*. New York: Free Press.

Pattillo-McCoy, Mary. 1999. *Black Picket Fences: Privilege and Peril Among the Black Middle Class*. Chicago and London: University of Chicago Press.

Perrucci, Robert and Earl Wysong. 2007. *New Class Society: Goodbye American Dream?* 3rd ed. Lanham, MD: Rowman & Littlefield.

———. 2008. *New Class Society: Goodbye American Dream?* 4th ed. Lanham, MD: Rowman & Littlefield.

Plantin, Lars. 2007. "Different Classes, Different Fathers? On Fatherhood and Economic Conditions in Sweden." *Community, Work, and Family* 10:93–110.

Rank, M. R. 2009. "Measuring the Economic Racial Divide Across the Course of American Lives." *Race and Social Problems* 1:57–66.

Reuter, Edward Byron and Jessie Ridgway Runner. 1931. *The Family: Source Materials for the Study of Family and Personality.* New York: McGraw-Hill.

Risman, Barbara. 1998. *Gender Vertigo: American Families in Transition.* New Haven and London: Yale University Press.

Robinson, William I. 2004. *A Theory of Global Capitalism: Production, Class, and the State in a Transnational World.* Baltimore, MD: Johns Hopkins University Press.

Roosa, Mark W., Shiying Deng, Rajni L. Nair and Ginger Lockhart Burrell. 2005. "Measures for Studying Poverty in Family and Child Research." *Journal of Marriage and the Family* 67:971–989.

Roschelle, Anne R. 1997. *No More Kin: Exploring Race,Class, and Gender in Family Networks.* Thousand Oaks, CA: Sage.

Rosenfeld, M. J. 2007. *The Age of Independence: Interracial Unions, Same-Sex Unions, and the Changing American Family.* Cambridge, MA: Harvard University Press.

Rossides, Daniel W. 1997. *Social Stratification: The Interplay of Class, Race, and Gender.* Upper Saddle River, NJ: Prentice Hall.

Rothbaum, F., M. Kakinuma, R. Nagaoka, and H. Azuma. 2007. "Attachment and Amae: Parent-Child Closeness in the United States and Japan." *Journal of Cross-Cultural Psychology* 38:465–486.

Royce, Edward. 2009. *Poverty and Power: The Problem of Structural Inequality.* Lanham, MD: Rowman & Littlefield.

Rubin, Lillian B. 1976. *Worlds of Pain: Life in the Working Class Family.* New York: Basic Books.

———. 1994. *Families on the Fault Line: America's Working Class Speaks About the Family, the Economy, Race, and Ethnicity.* New York: HarperCollins.

Rury, John and Shirley A. Hill. *Closing the Achievement Gap: The African-American Struggle for High School Education, 1940–1980.*Unpublished Manuscript.

Ryscavage, Paul. 2009. *Rethinking the Income Gap.* New Brunswick, NJ: Transaction.

Sakamoto, Arthur, Kimberly A. Goyette, and ChangHawn Kim. 2009. "Socioeconomic Attainments of Asian Americans." *Annual Review of Sociology* 35:255–276.

Sanday, P. R. 1981. *Female Power and Male Dominance: On the Origins of Sexual Inequality.* Cambridge, MA: Cambridge University Press.

Sarkisian, Natalia, Mariana Gerena, and Naomi Gerstel. 2007. "Extended Family Integration Among Euro and Mexican Americans: Ethnicity, Gender, and Class." *Journal of Marriage and the Family* 69:40–54.

Sarkisian, Natalia and Naomi Gerstel. 2004. "Kin Support Among Blacks and Whites: Race and Family Organization." *American Sociological Review* 69:812–837.

Savin-Williams, Ruth C. and Kristin G. Esterberg. 2000. "Lesbian, Gay, and Bisexual Families." Pp. 197–215 in *Handbook of Family Diversity,* edited by D. H. Demo, Katherine R. Allen, and Mark A. Fine. New York: Oxford University Press.

Schaefer, Richard T. 2008. *Racial and Ethnic Groups*. Upper Saddle River, NJ: Pearson Prentice Hall.

Schwartz, Jennifer. 2006. "Effects of Diverse Forms of Family Structure on Female and Male Homicide." *Journal of Marriage and the Family* 68:1291–1312.

Scott, Ellen K., Andrew S. London, and Nancy A. Myers. 2002. "Dangerous Dependencies: The Intersection of Welfare Reform and Domestic Violence." *Gender & Society* 16:878–897.

Seccombe, Karen. 2007. *Families in Poverty*. New York: Pearson Education.

Seccombe, Karen and Rebecca L. Warner. 2004. *Marriages and Families: Relationships in Social Context*. Belmont, CA: Wadsworth/Thomson.

Sennett, Richard. 1973. *The Hidden Injuries of Class*. New York: Vintage Books.

——. 1974. *Families Against the City: Middle-Class Homes of Industrial Chicago, 1872–1890*. New York: Vintage Books.

Sennett, Richard and Jonathan Cobb. 1972. *Hidden Injuries of Class*. New York: Vintage.

Sernau, Scott. 2011. *Social Inequality in a Global Age*. Thousand Oaks, CA: Pine Forge Press.

Shlain, Leonard. 2003. *Sex, Time, and Power: How Women's Sexuality Shaped Human Evolution*. London: Penguin Books.

Sigle-Rushton, Wendy and Sara McLanahan. 2004. "Father Absence and Child Well-Being: A Critical Review." Pp. 116–155 in *Future of the Family*, edited by D. P. Moynihan, T. M. Smeeding, and L. Rainwater. New York: Russell Sage Foundation.

Sprey, Jetse. 1979. "Conflict Theory and the Study of Marriage and the Family." Pp. 130–159 in *Contemporary Theories About the Family: General Theories/Theoretical Orientations*, vol. 2, edited by W. R. Burr, R. Hill, F. I. Nye, and I. L. Reiss. New York: Free Press.

Stack, Carol. 1974. *All Our Kin: Strategies for Survival in a Black Community*. New York: Harper & Row.

Steinberg, Stephen. 2001. *The Ethnic Myth: Race, Ethnicity, and Class in America*. Boston: Beacon Press.

Stiglitz, Joseph E. 2007. *Making Globalization Work*. New York: W. W. Norton.

Straus, Murray A., Richard J. Gelles, and Suzanne K. Steinmetz. 1980. *Behind Closed Doors: Violence in the American Family*. New York: Doubleday.

Straus, Murray A., with Denise Donnelly. 1994. *Beating the Devil Out of Them: Corporal Punishment in American Families*. San Francisco: Jossey-Bass.

Strong, Bryan, Christine DeVault, and Theodore F. Cohen. 2008. *Marriage and Family Experience: Intimate Relationships in a Changing Society*. Belmont, CA: Thomson Wadsworth.

Sudarkasa, Niara. 1996. *The Strength of Our Mothers: African & African American Women and Families: Essays and Speeches*. Trenton, NJ: Africa World Press.

Sullivan, Oriel. 2006. *Changing Gender Relations, Changing Families: Tracing the Pace of Change Over Time*. Lanham, MD: Rowman & Littlefield.

Taylor, R. J., L. M. Chatters, M. B. Tucker, and D. Lewis. 1990. "Developments in Research on Black Families: A Decade Review." *Journal of Marriage and the Family* 52:993–1014.

Thornton, Arland. 2005. *Reading History Sideways: The Fallacy and Enduring Impact of the Developmental Paradigm on Family Life*. Chicago: University of Chicago Press.

Thornton, Arland, William G. Axinn, and Yu Xie. 2007. *Marriage and Cohabitation*. Chicago: University of Chicago Press.

Tichenor, Veronica Jaris. 2005. *Earning More and Getting Less: Why Successful Women Can't Buy Equality*. New Brunswick, NJ: Rutgers University Press.

Tilly, Charles. 2005. "Historical Perspectives on Inequality." Pp. 15–30 in *The Blackwell Companion to Social Inequalities,* edited by M. Romero and E. Margolis. Malden, MA: Blackwell.

Truxal, Andrew G. and Francis E. Merrill. 1947. *Family in American Culture*. New York: Prentice Hall.

Uchitelle, Louis. 2000, September 10. "Working Families Strain to Live Middle-Class Life." *The New York Times* (http://www.nytimes.com).

U.S. Census Bureau. 2009. "Income, Poverty and Health Insurance Coverage in the United States: 2008." Washington, DC: Public Information Office. (http://www.census.gov/newsroom/releases/archives/income_wealth/cb09-141.html)

Vecker, Jeremy E. and Charlene E. Stokes. 2008. "Early Marriage in the United States." *Journal of Marriage and the Family* 70:835–846.

Waite, Linda and Maggie Gallagher. 2000. *The Case for Marriage: Why Married People are Happier, Healthier and Better Off Financially*. New York: Doubleday.

Wallerstein, Immanuel. 2004. *World-Systems Analysis: An Introduction*. Durham, NC: Duke University Press.

Walsh, L. 1985. "The Experiences and Status of Women in the Chesapeake." Pp. 1–18 in *The Web of Southern Social Relations: Women, Family, and Education,* edited by W. Fraser, R. F. Saunders, and J. Wakelyn. Athens: University of Georgia Press.

Warner, Lloyd. 1949. *Social Class in America*. Chicago: Science Research Associates.

Warren, Elizabeth and Amelia Warren Tyagi. 2003. *The Two-Income Trap: Why Middle-Class Mothers and Fathers Are Going Broke*. New York: Basic Books.

Weitzman, Lenore J. 1981. *The Marriage Contract*. New York: Free Press.

Wilson, William J. 1978. *The Declining Significance of Race: Blacks and Changing American Institutions*. Chicago: University of Chicago Press.

Wilson, W. J. 1987. *The Truly Disadvantaged*. Chicago: University of Chicago Press.

———. 2006. "Jobless Poverty: A New Form of Social Dislocation in the Inner-City Ghetto." Pp. 87–101 in *Inequality: Classic Readings in Race, Class, and Gender,* edited by D. B. Gruskey and S. Szelenyi. Boulder, CO: Westview.

Winant, Howard. 2001. *The World is a Ghetto: Race and Democracy Since World War II*. New York: Basic Books.

Wright, E. O. 1997. *Class Counts: Comparative Studies in Class Analysis*. Cambridge: Cambridge University Press.

Wright, Erik Olin. 2008. "Logics of Class Analysis." Pp. 329–349 in *Social Class: How Does It Work?* edited by A. Lareau and D. Conley. New York: Russell Sage Foundation.

Yalom, Marilyn. 2001. *A History of the Wife.* New York: HarperCollins.

Young, Alford. 2004. *The Lives of Marginalized Black Men: Making Sense of Mobility, Opportunity, and Future Life Chances.* Princeton, NJ: Princeton University Press.

Zinn, Howard. [1980] 2003. *A People's History of the United States: 1492–Present.* New York: HarperCollins.

Zinn, Maxine Baca and Bonnie Thornton Dill. 1996. "Theorizing Difference from Multiracial Feminism." *Feminist Studies* 22:321–331.

Zinn, Maxine Baca and D. Stanley Eitzen. 2002. *Diversity in Families.* Boston: Allyn and Bacon.

Zweigenhaft, Richard L. and G. William Domhoff. 2007. "Women in the Power Elite." Pp. 201–207 in *Understanding Inequality: The Intersection of Race/ Ethnicity, Class, and Gender*, edited by B. A. Arrighi. Lanham, MD: Rowman & Littlefield.

Index

Accomplishment by natural growth, 85, 106
Acker, Joan, 41
African American families, 16–18, 45–47. *See also* Race
Agricultural societies, settled, 6–7
Aldrich, Nelson, 67
Amato, Paul, 77
American Dilemma, An (Myrdal), xxiii
American Story, An (Dickerson), 71
Authoritarian parenting, 84
Authoritative parenting, 84

Baltzell, E. Digby, 54, 68
Beal, Frances, 43
Bernard, Jesse, 62, 78
Billingsley, Andrew, 47
Blue-Collar Aristocrats (LeMasters), 94
Blumer, Herbert, 35
Bobo Establishment, 58
Boston Brahmins, 59
Brewer, Rose, 43
Brooks, David, 56
Browne, Irene, 98
Burgess, Ernest, 37

Carnegie, Andrew, 60
Caste pluralism, xxii
Cherlin, Andrew, xx, 77
Children
    having and rearing, 82–86, 105–107
    in single-parent families, 109–112
    socializing, in elite and upper-class families, 64–68
Chinese Exclusion Act, 20

Class
    inequality, and the post-industrial economy, 27–28
    warfare, xxviii
    See also Social class
Class Matters, 61
Coleman, James, 65
Collins, P. H., 42
Colonial America, social inequalities in, 12–18
Comte, August, 30
Concerted cultivation, 85, 106
Conflict theory, 31, 37–39
Conley, Dalton, 76
Conwell, Russell, 95
Coontz, Stephanie, 75
Core nations, 119
Cox, Oliver, 44
Cult of true womanhood, 24, 74
Culture
    resurgence of, 97–99
    social class and, 47–49
Culture of poverty, 95
Culture of strength, 107
Culture-structure nexus, 95–97

Dabel, Jane, 17
Darwin, Charles, 30
Davis, Kingsley, 33
de Tocqueville, Alexis, 72
Death of Class, The (Pakulski and Waters), 124
Dewey, John, 35
Dickerson, Debra, 71
Doctrine of separate spheres, 23, 73–74

145

About the Author

Shirley A. Hill is a professor of sociology at the University of Kansas, where she studies family diversity, social inequality, and health care. She is the author of *Race, Work, and Family: New Century Values Among African American Men and Women* (co-edited with Marlese Durr; Rowman & Littlefield, 2006); *Black Intimacies: A Gender Perspective on Families and Relationships* (AltaMira, 2005); *African American Children: Their Socialization and Development in Families* (Sage, 1999); and other books and articles. Her current research focuses on racial disparities in educational attainment.

SAGE Research Methods Online

The essential tool for researchers

**Sign up now at
www.sagepub.com/srmo
for more information.**

An expert research tool!

- An **expertly designed taxonomy** with more than 1,400 unique terms for social and behavioral science research methods

- **Visual and hierarchical search tools** to help you discover material and link to related methods

- Easy-to-use navigation tools
- Content organized by complexity
- Tools for citing, printing, and downloading content with ease
- Regularly updated content and features

A wealth of essential content

- The most comprehensive picture of quantitative, qualitative, and mixed methods available today

- More than **100,000 pages of SAGE book and reference material** on research methods as well as editorially selected material from SAGE journals

- More than **600 books** available in their entirety online

Launching 2011!